GOSPEL SONGS OF JOHNNY CASH

E-Z Play TODAY is designed for you!

- All songs are arranged for use with all major brand organs.
- Special chord notation for SINGLE KEY CHORDS . . . TRIAD CHORDS . . . and STANDARD CHORD POSITIONS.
- The result. . .INSTANT PLAYING ENJOYMENT!

Contents

7777 W. Bluemound Rd. P.O. Box 13819 Milwaukee, WI 53213

My God Is Real
(Yes, God Is Real)

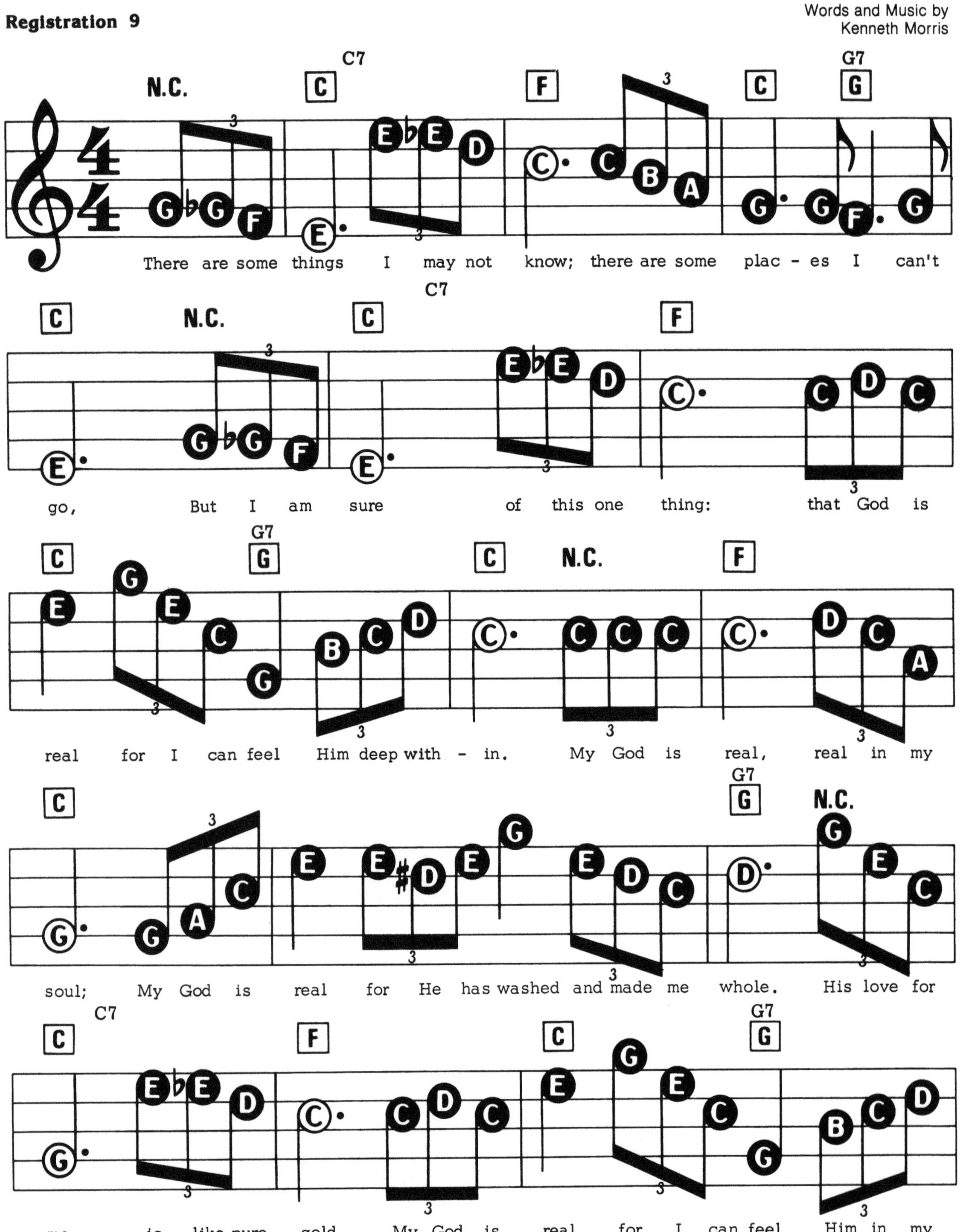

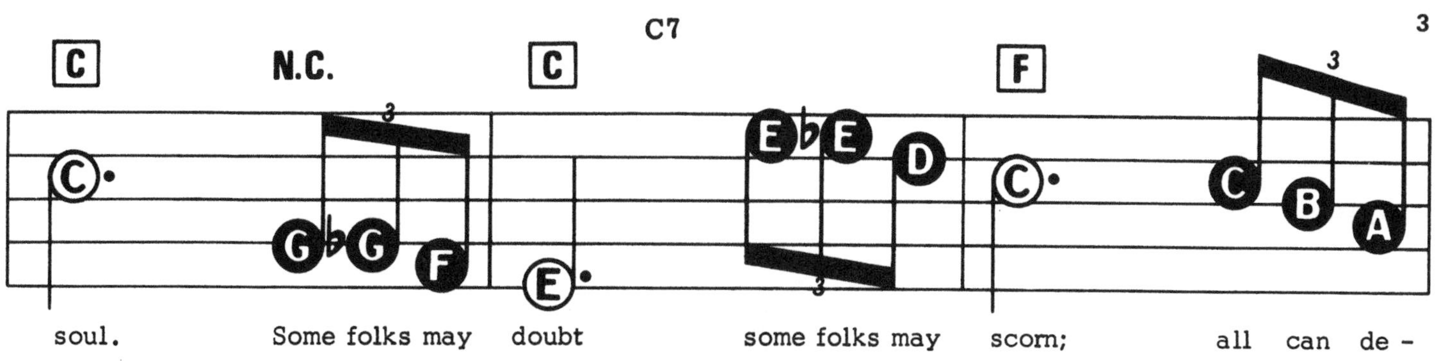
C
N.C.
C7
C
F
soul. Some folks may doubt some folks may scorn; all can de -

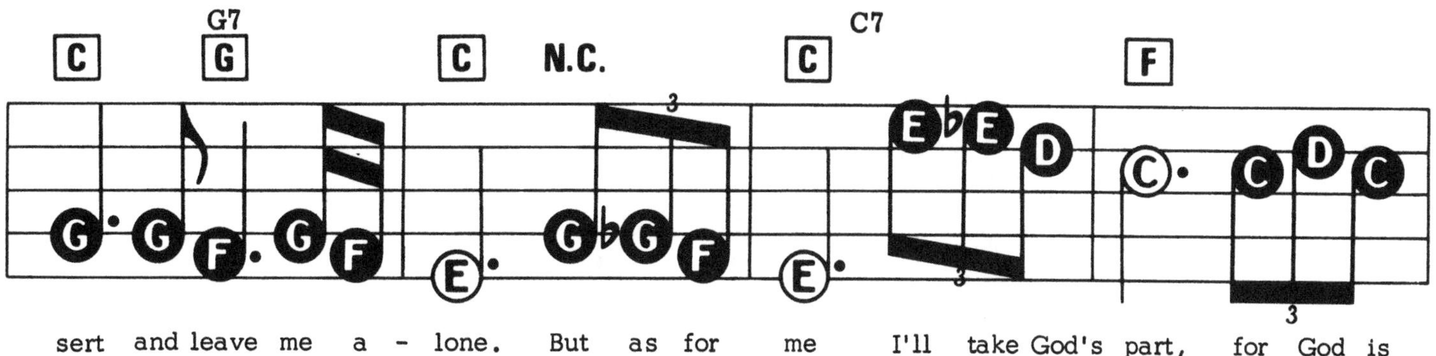
C
G7
G
C
N.C.
C7
C
F
sert and leave me a - lone. But as for me I'll take God's part, for God is

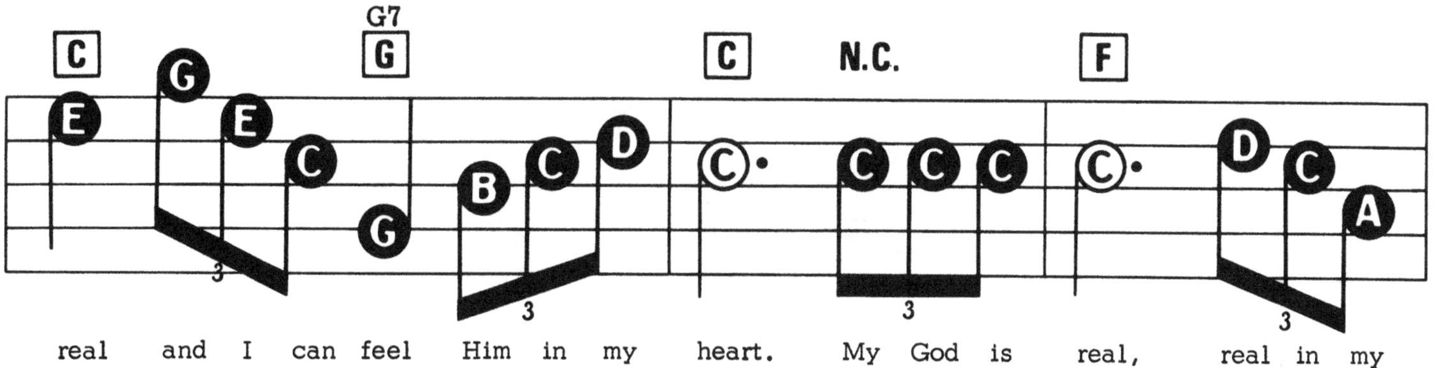
C
G7
G
C
N.C.
F
real and I can feel Him in my heart. My God is real, real in my

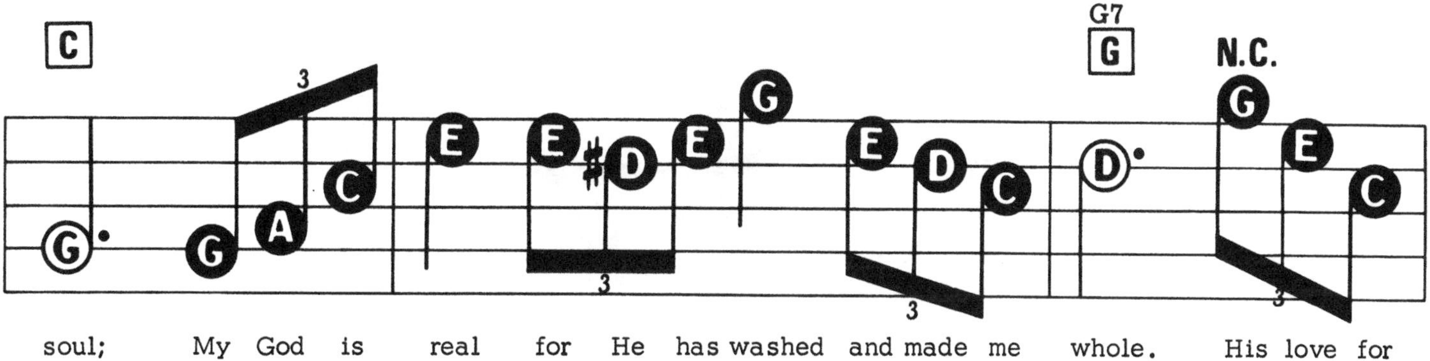
C
G7
G
N.C.
soul; My God is real for He has washed and made me whole. His love for

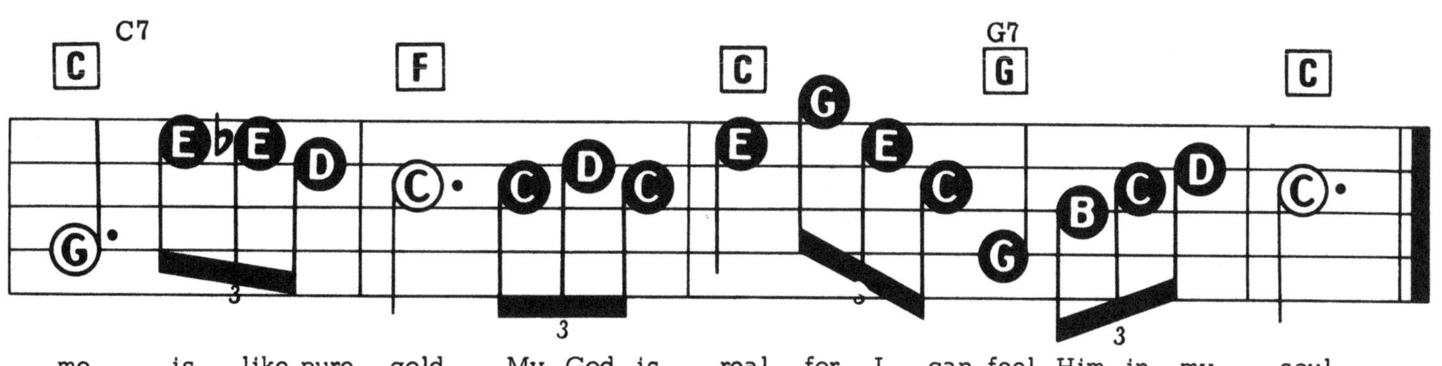
C7
C
F
C
G7
G
C
me is like pure gold. My God is real for I can feel Him in my soul.

Swing Low, Sweet Chariot

Registration 4

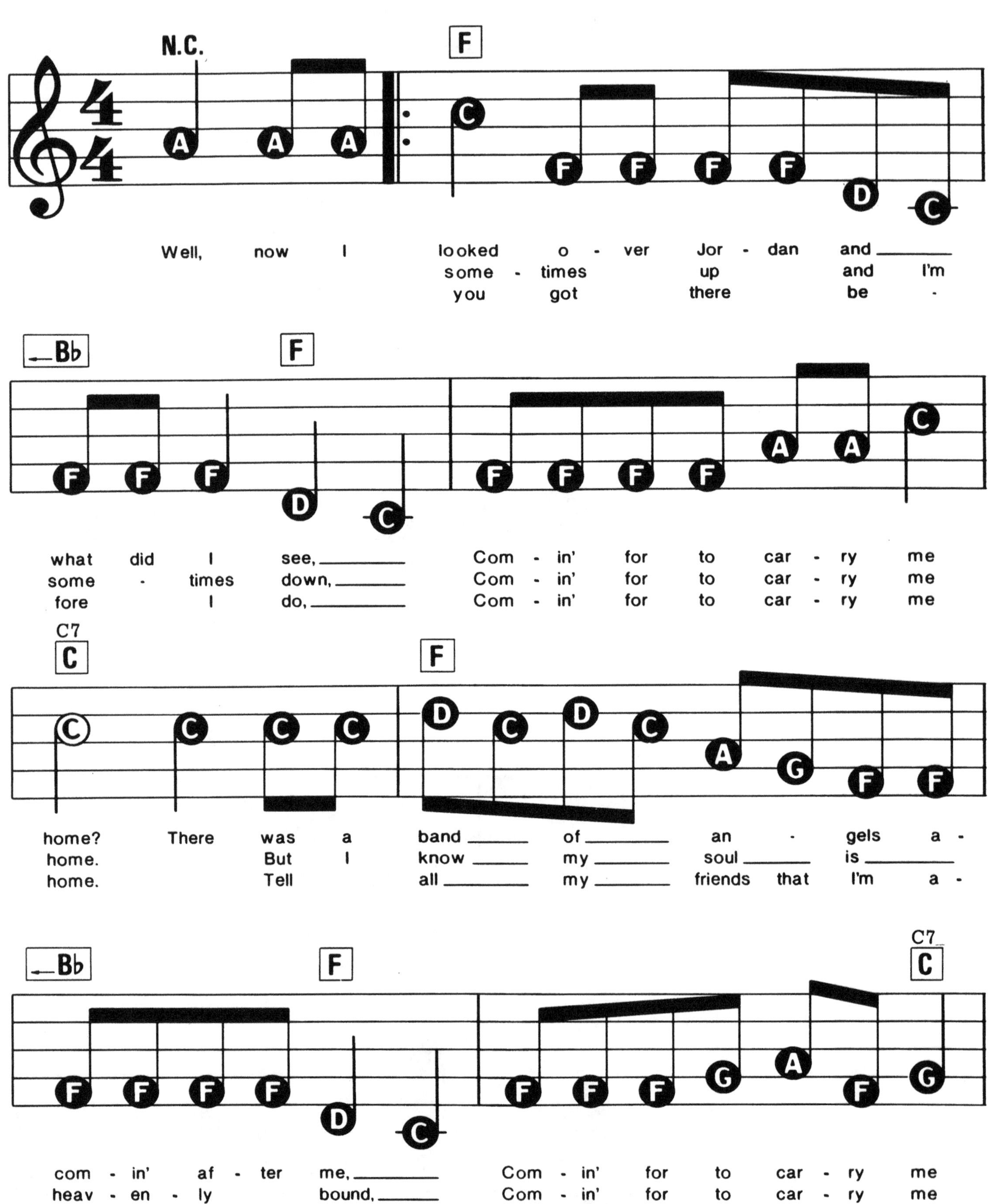

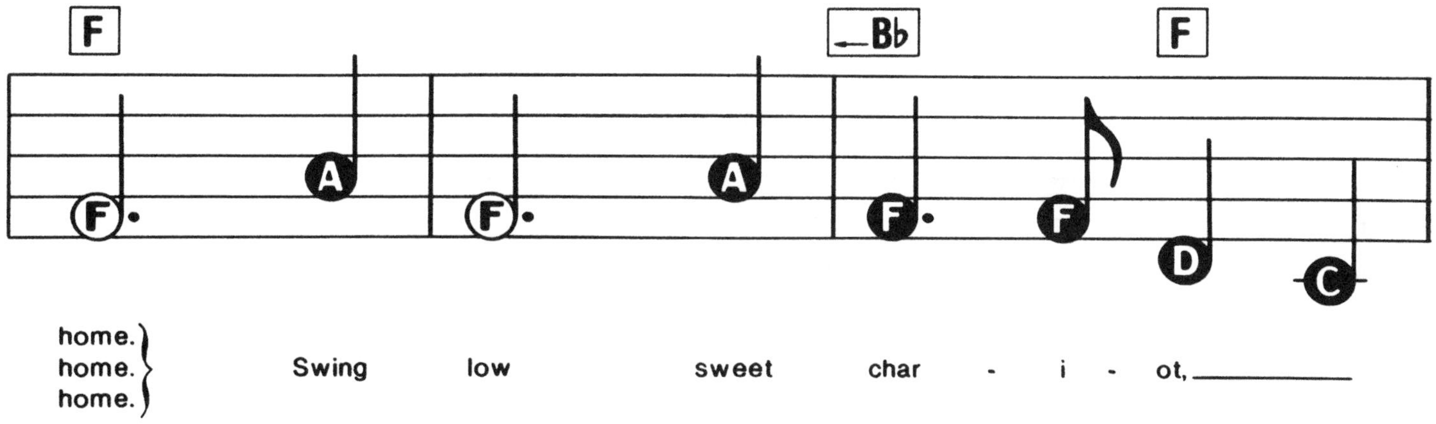
F
Bb
F
F
A
F
A
F
F
D
C
home.
home.
home.
Swing low sweet char - i - ot,

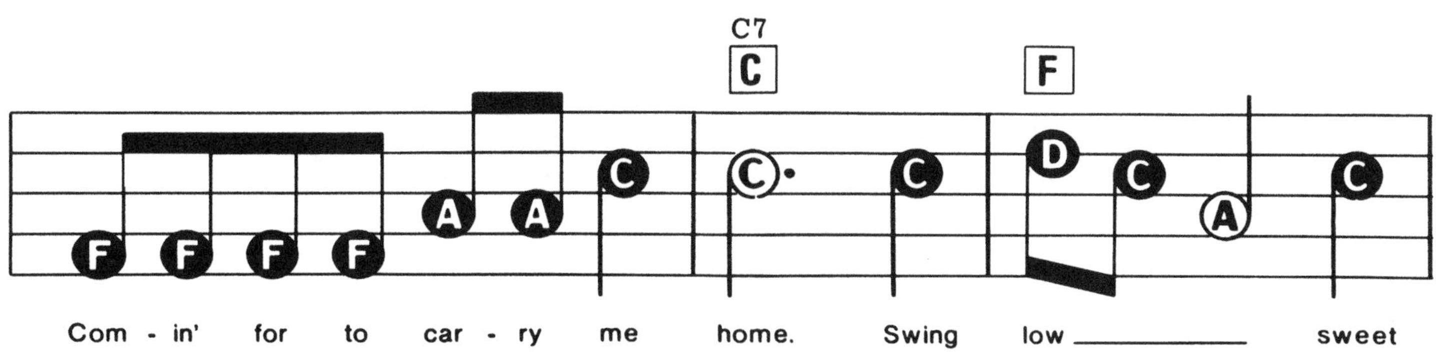
C7
C
F
F F F F A A C C C D C A C
Com - in' for to car - ry me home. Swing low sweet

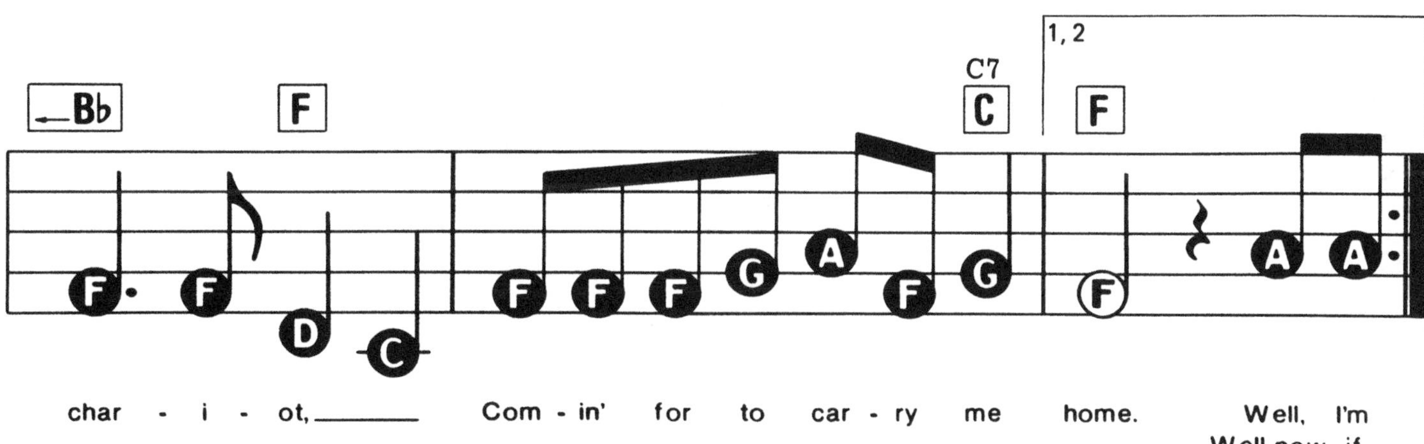
1, 2
Bb
F
C7
C
F
F F D C F F F G A F G F A A
char - i - ot, Com - in' for to car - ry me home. Well, I'm
Well, now if

3
F
C7
C
F
F F F D F F F G A F G F
home. Well, now they're com - in' for to car - ry me home

New Born Man

Registration 7

Words and Music by
Johnny Cash and John Carter Cash

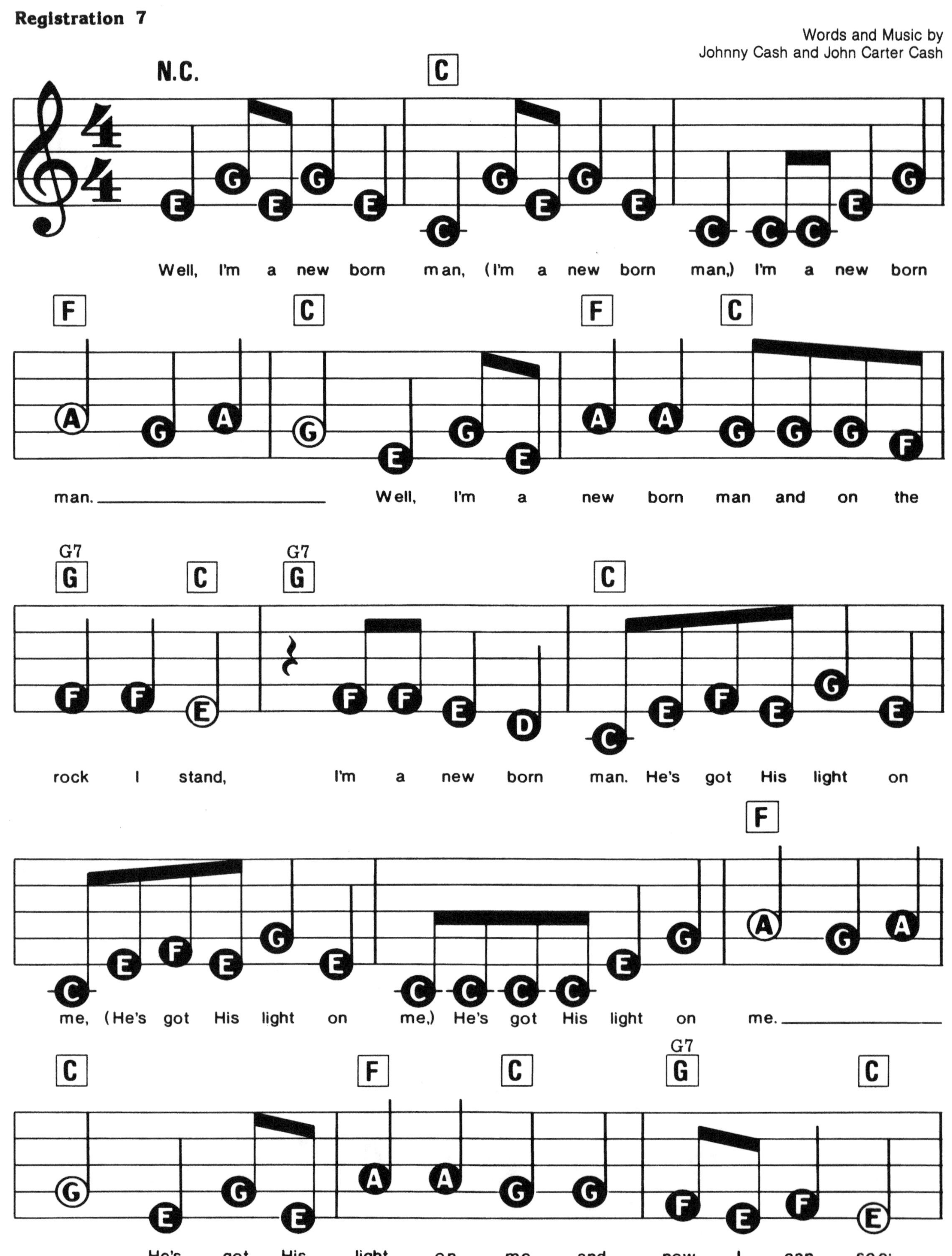

G7 G C
He's got His light on me. He loves me all of the time, (He loves me all of the
F C
time,) He loves me all of the time. He loves me
F C G7 G C G7 G
all of the time, He lets me know He's mine; He loves me all of the
C
time. I'm a new born man, (I'm a new born man,) I'm a new born
F C F C
man. Well, I'm a new born man and on the

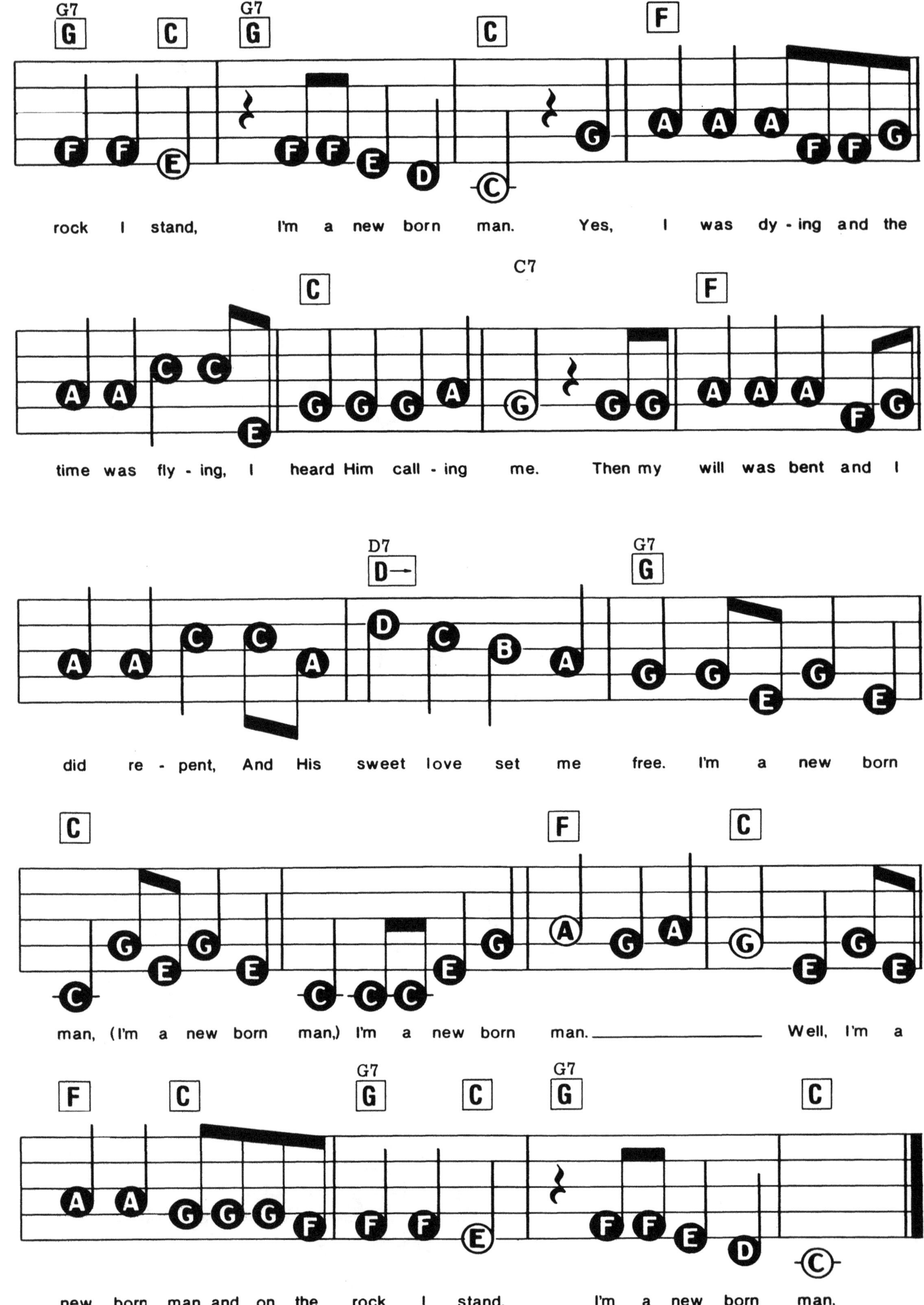
G7 G C G7 G C F
rock I stand, I'm a new born man. Yes, I was dy - ing and the
C C7 F
time was fly - ing, I heard Him call - ing me. Then my will was bent and I
D7 D G7 G
did re - pent, And His sweet love set me free. I'm a new born
C F C
man, (I'm a new born man,) I'm a new born man. Well, I'm a
F C G7 G C G7 G C
new born man and on the rock I stand, I'm a new born man.

Greystone Chapel

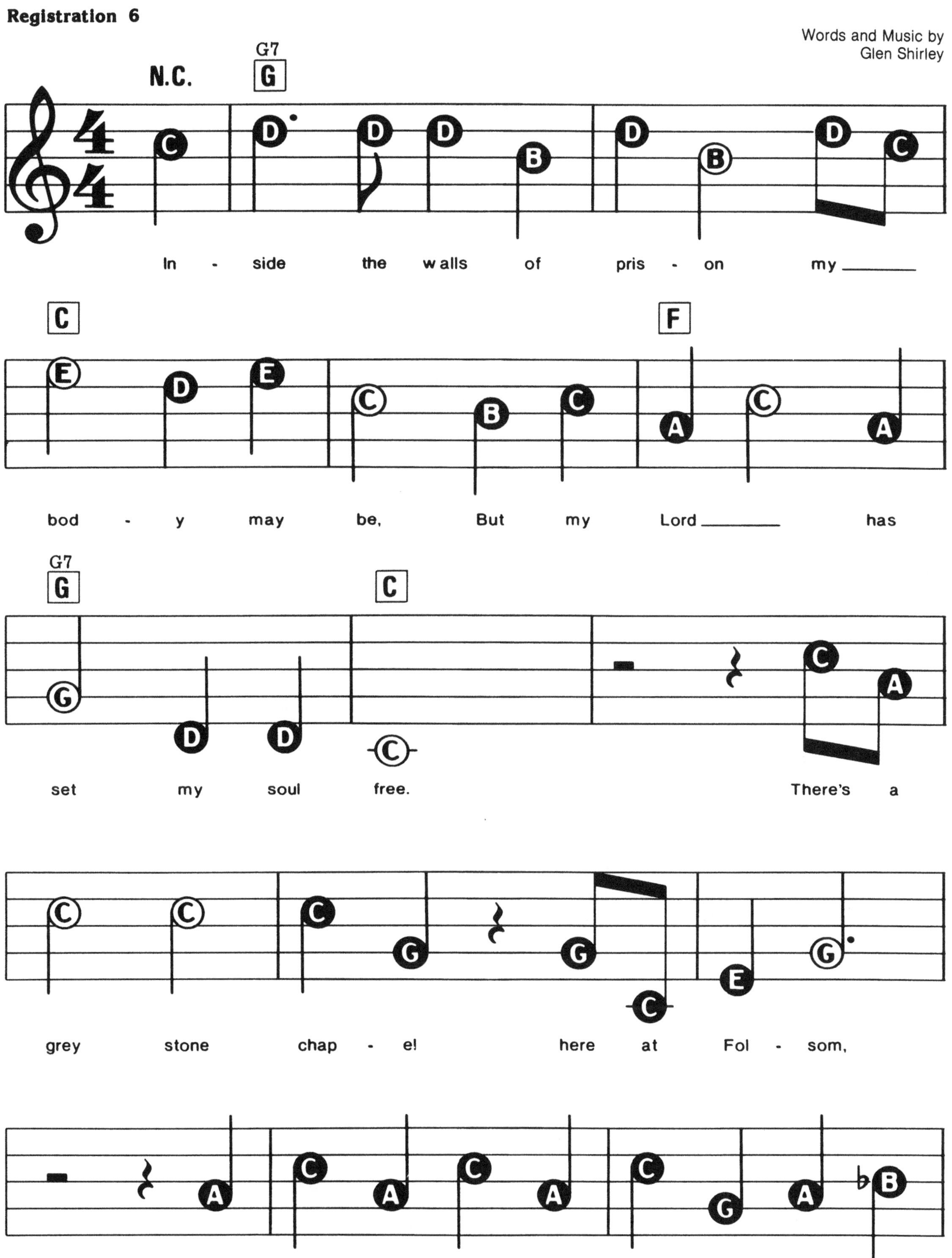

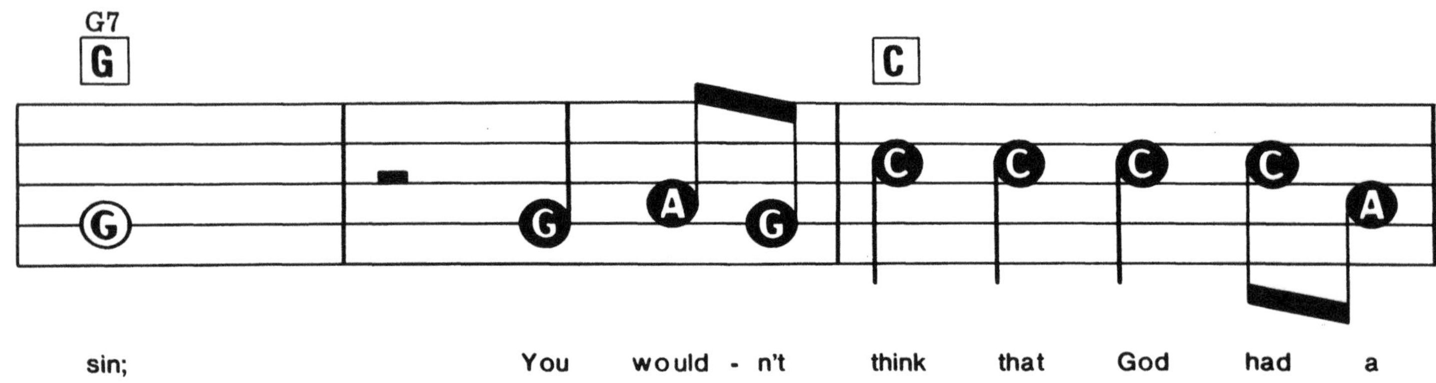
G7
G
C
G
G
A
G
C
C
C
C
A
sin; You would - n't think that God had a

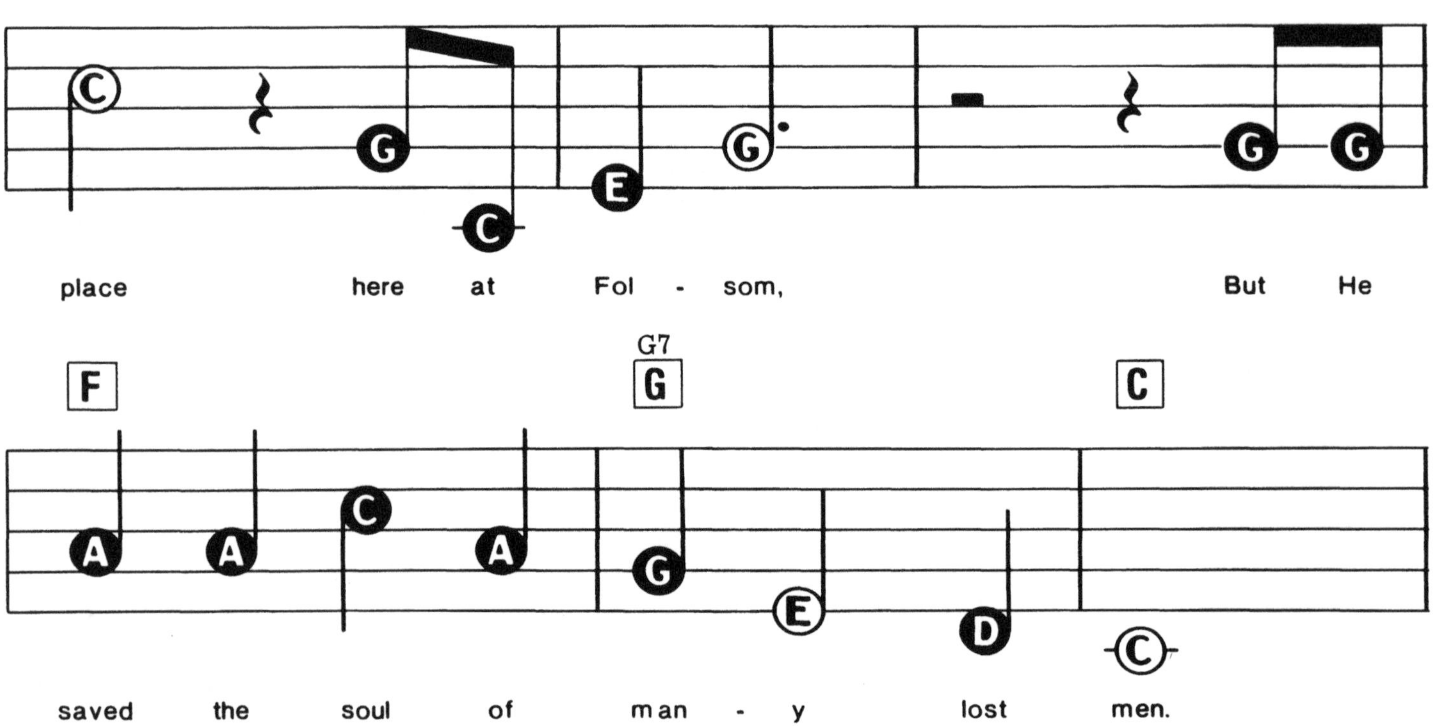
C
G
C
E
G
G
G
place here at Fol - som, But He
F
G7
G
C
A
A
C
A
G
E
D
C
saved the soul of man - y lost men.

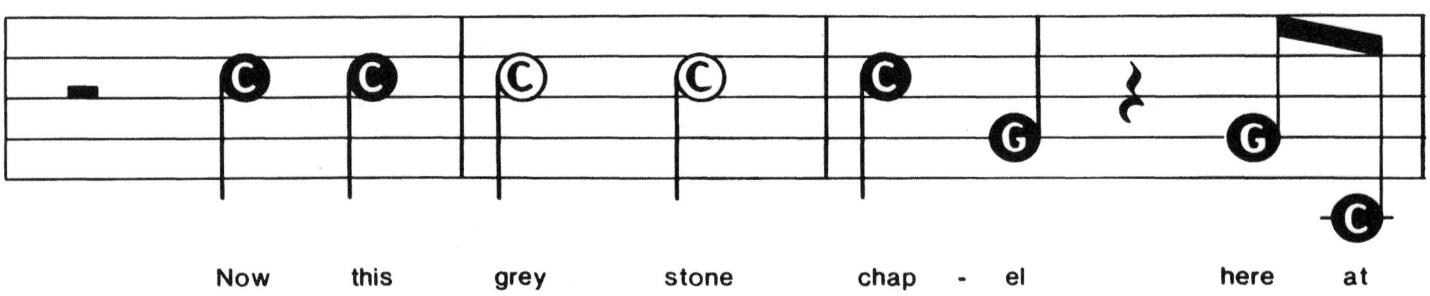
C
C
C
C
C
G
G
C
Now this grey stone chap - el here at

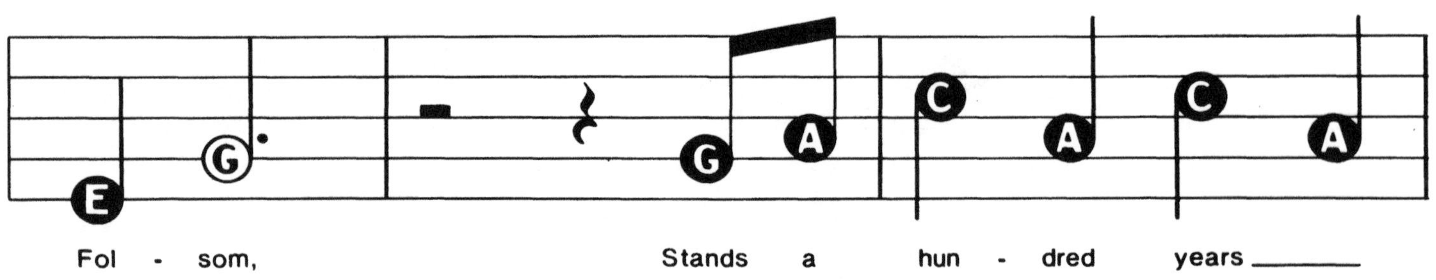
E
G
G
A
C
A
C
A
Fol - som, Stands a hun - dred years

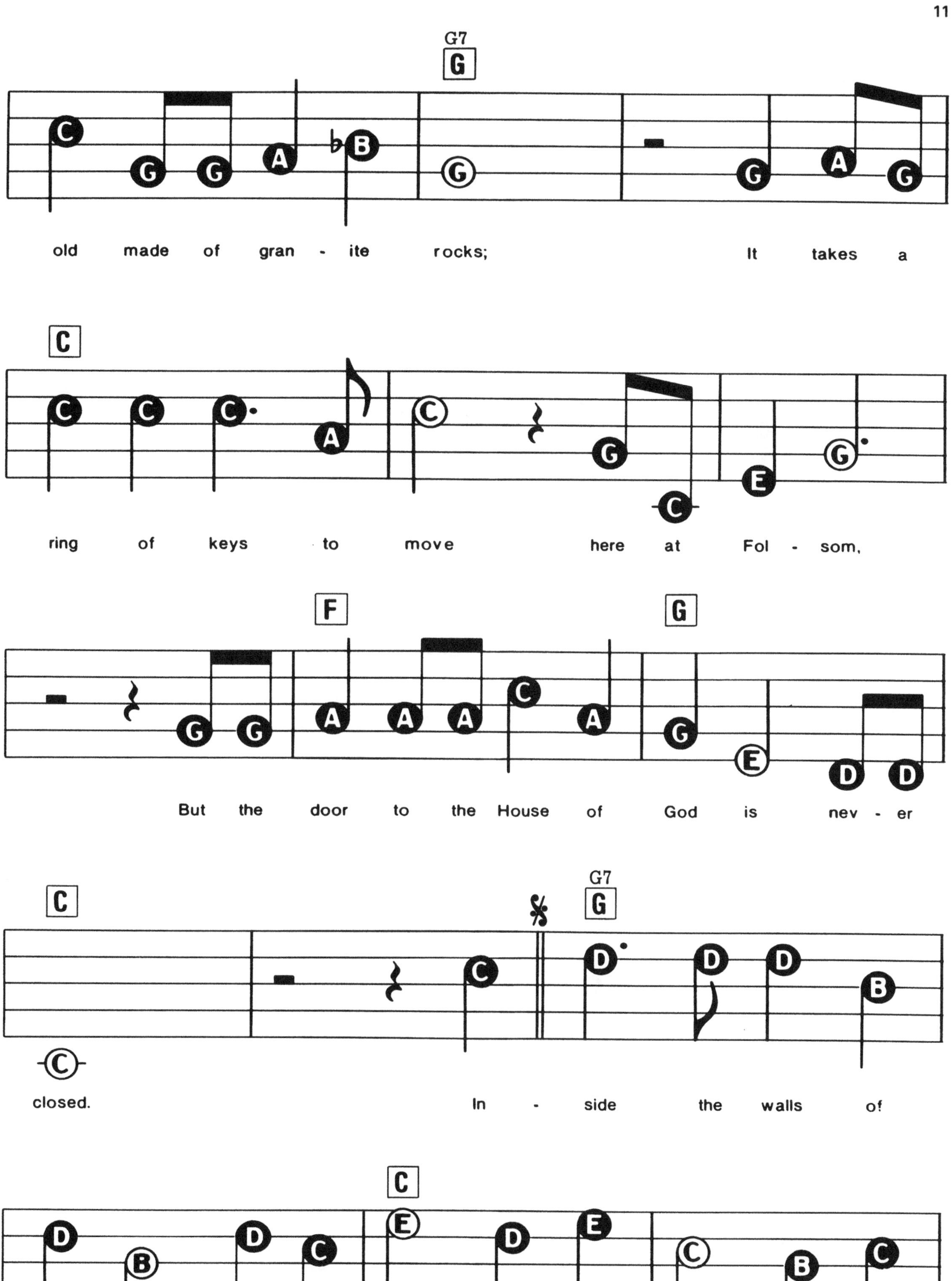
G7
G
C
old made of gran - ite rocks;
It takes a
C
ring of keys to move
here at Fol - som,
F
G
But the door to the House of God is nev - er
C
G7
G
closed.
In - side the walls of
C
pris - on my bod - y may be,
But my

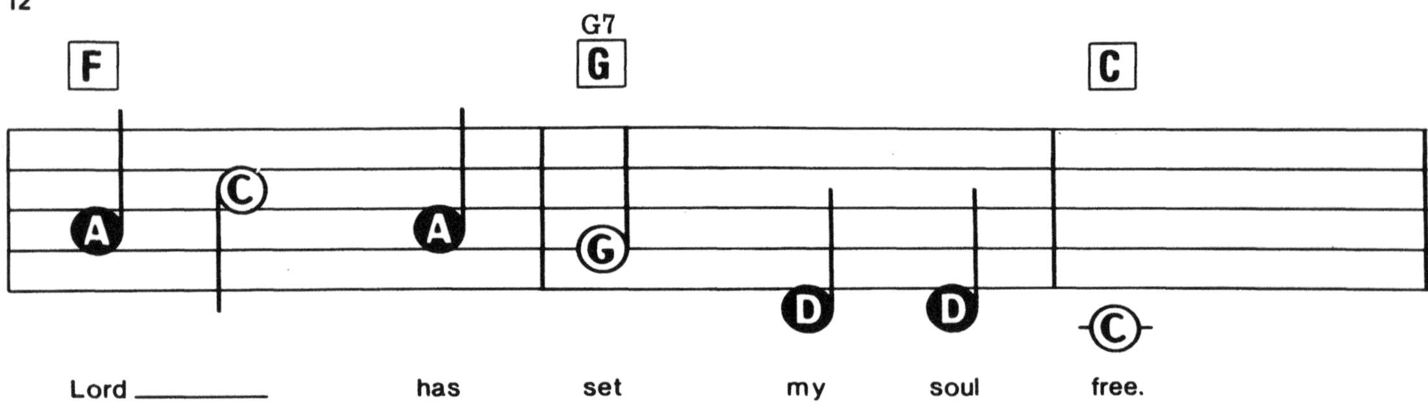
G7
F
G
C
Lord ___ has set my soul free.

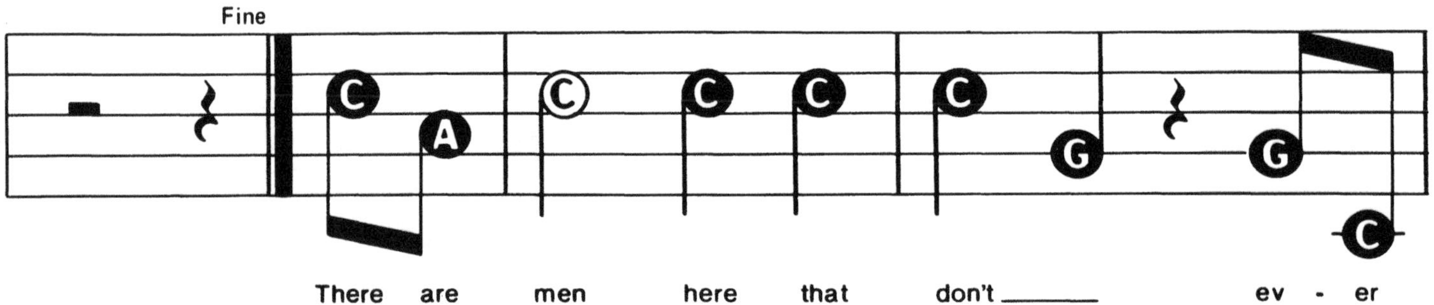
Fine
There are men here that don't ___ ev - er

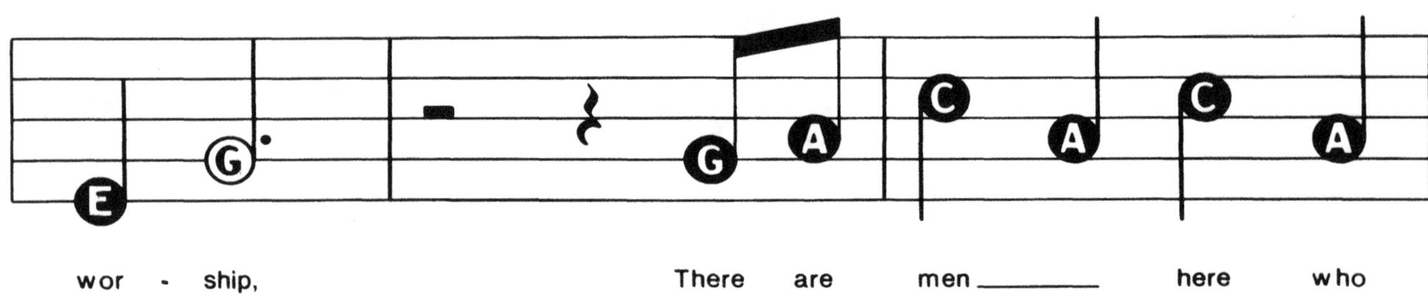
wor - ship,
There are men ___ here who

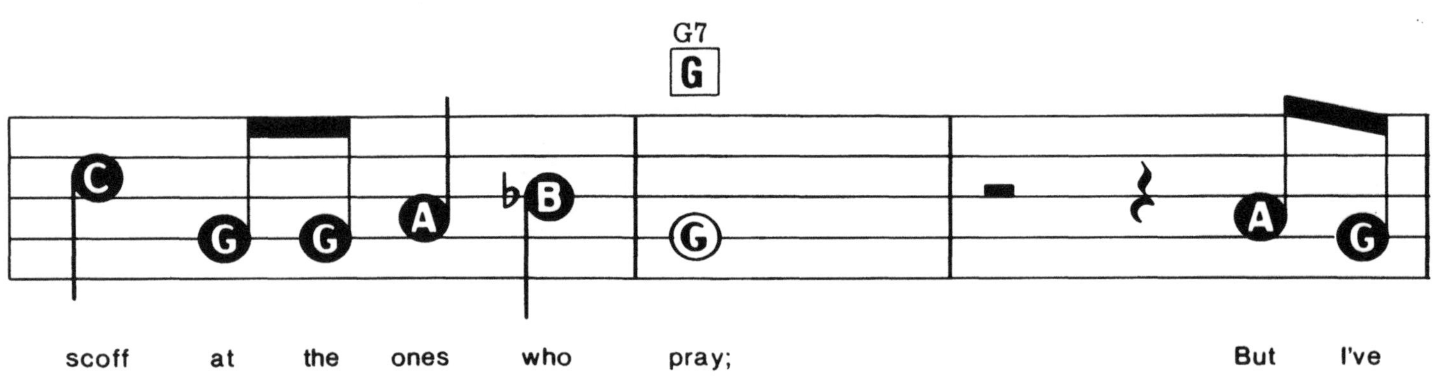
G7
G
scoff at the ones who pray;
But I've

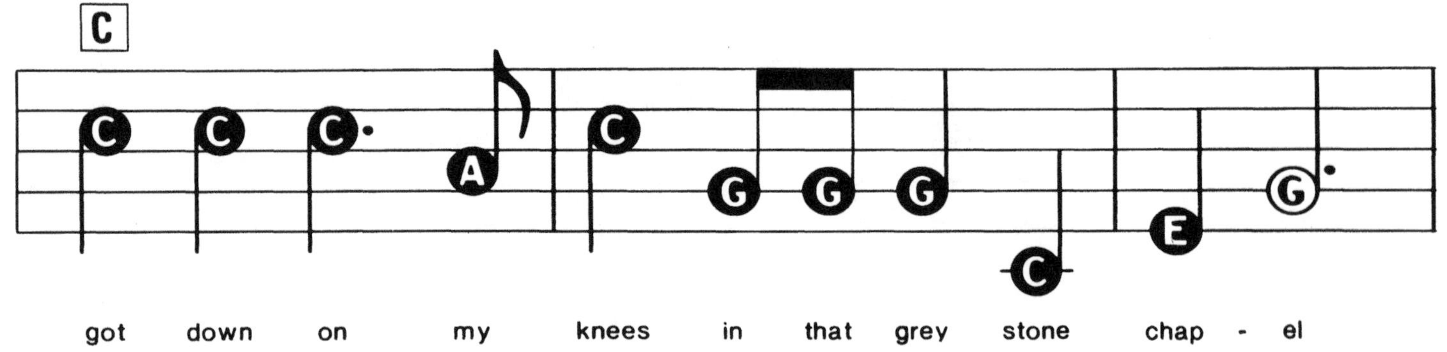
C
got down on my knees in that grey stone chap - el

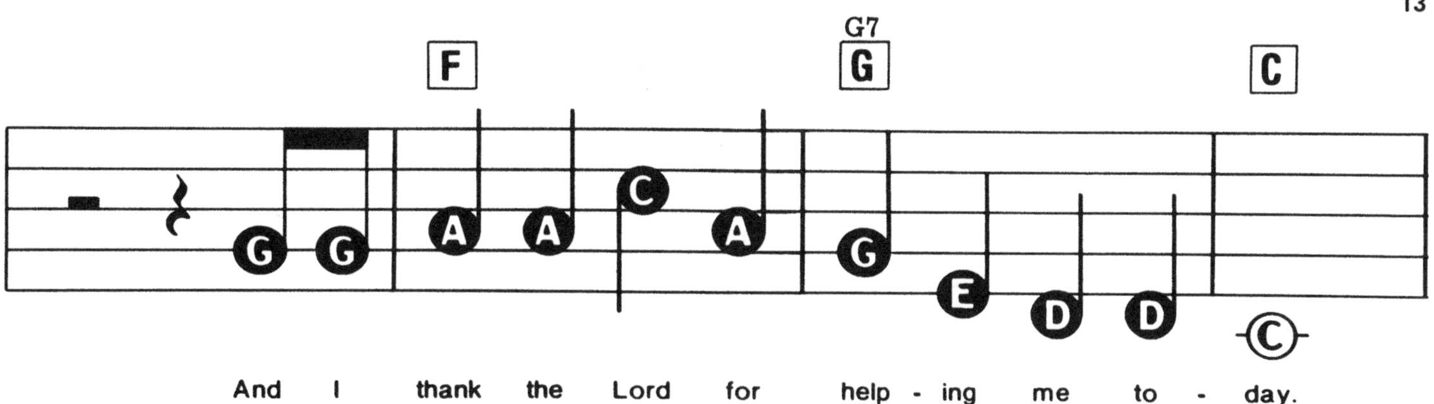
F
G7
G
C
G G A A C A G E D D C
And I thank the Lord for help - ing me to - day.

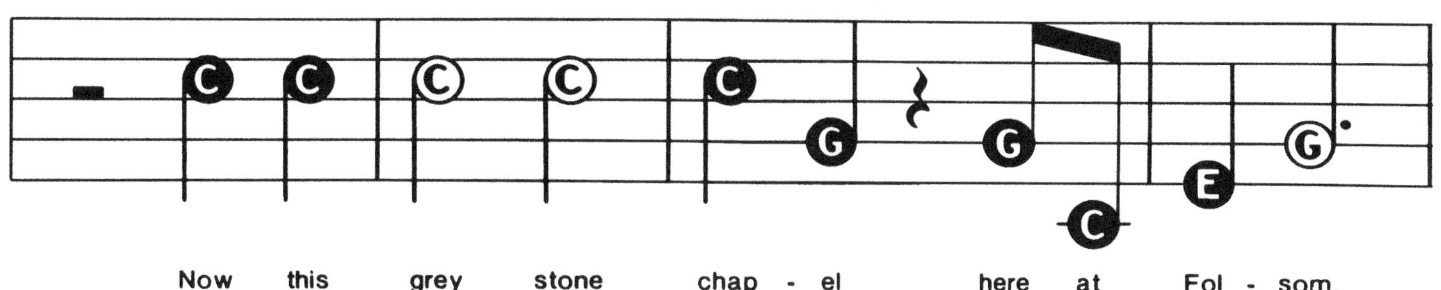
C C C C C G G C E G
Now this grey stone chap - el here at Fol - som,

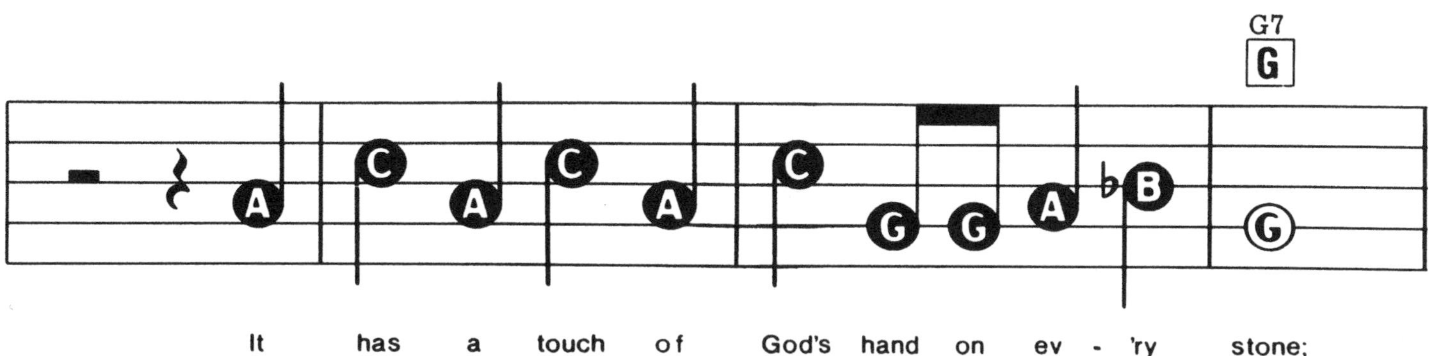
G7
G
A C A C A C G G A B G
It has a touch of God's hand on ev - 'ry stone;

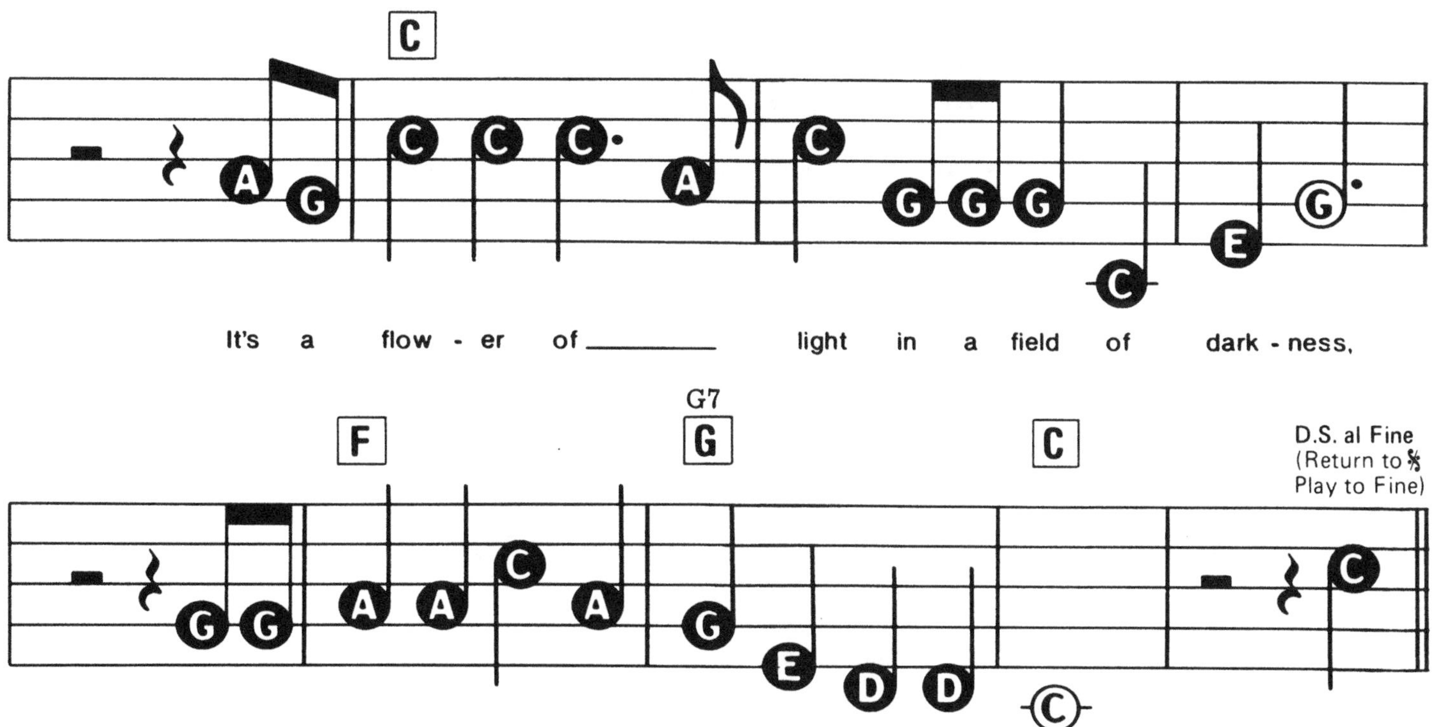
C
A G C C C A C G G G C E G
It's a flow - er of light in a field of dark - ness,
F
G7
G
C
D.S. al Fine
(Return to 𝄋
Play to Fine)
G G A A C A G E D D C C
And it's giv - en me the strength to car - ry on. In -

Land Of Israel

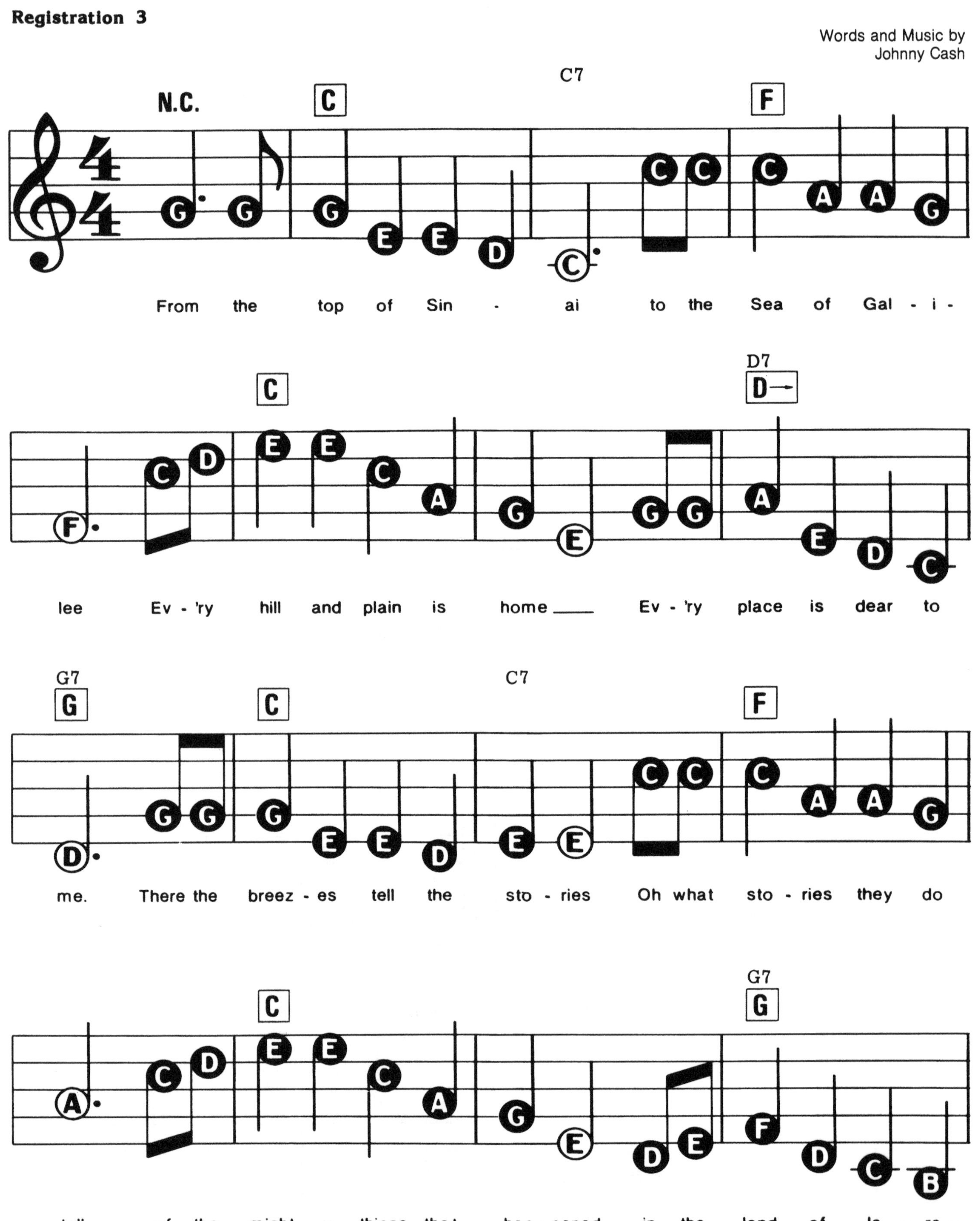

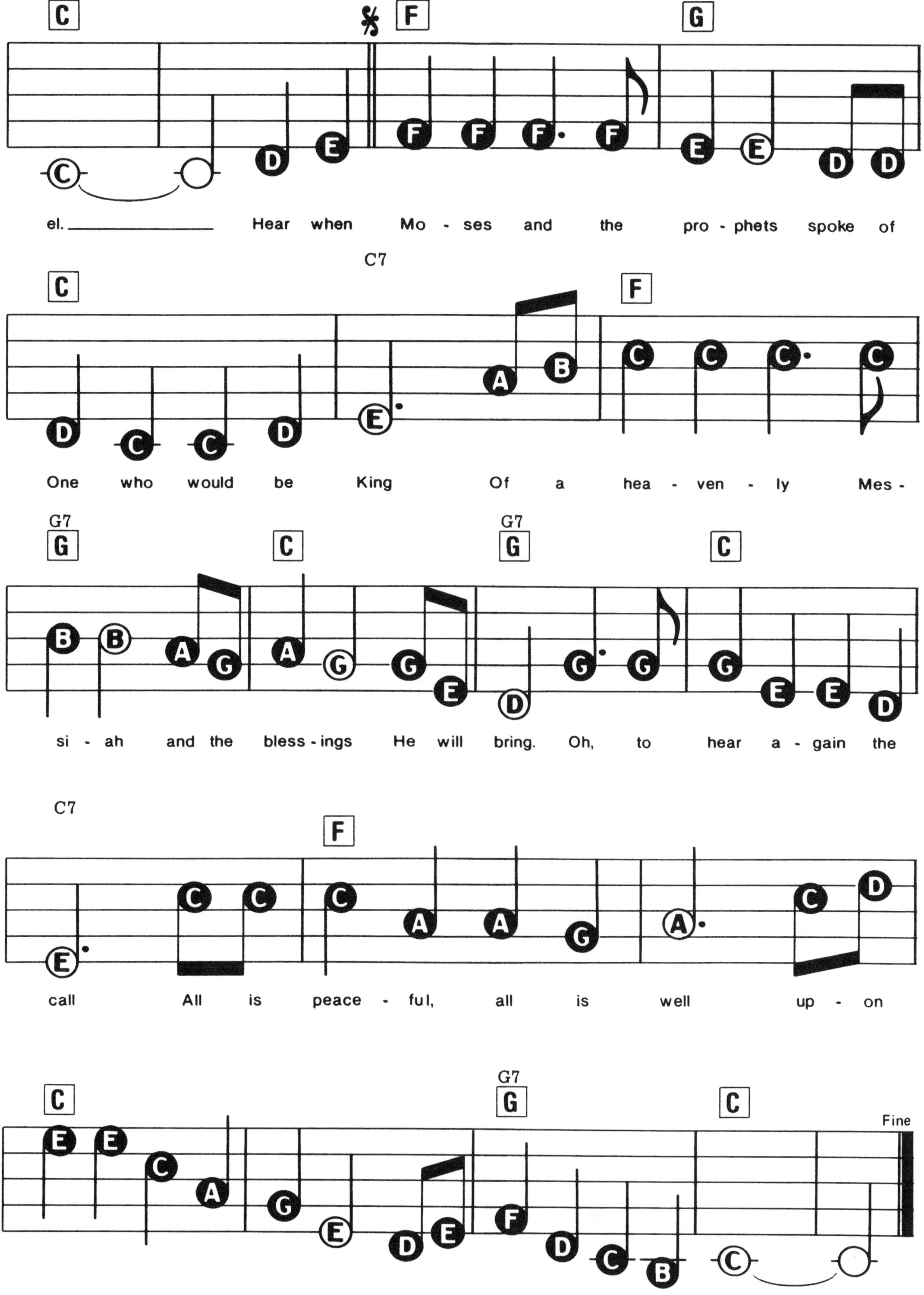
C F G
el. Hear when Mo - ses and the pro - phets spoke of
C C7 F
One who would be King Of a hea - ven - ly Mes -
G7 G C G7 G C
si - ah and the bless - ings He will bring. Oh, to hear a - gain the
C7 F
call All is peace - ful, all is well up - on
C G7 G C
Fine
ev - 'ry rock and moun - tain in the land of Is - ra - el.

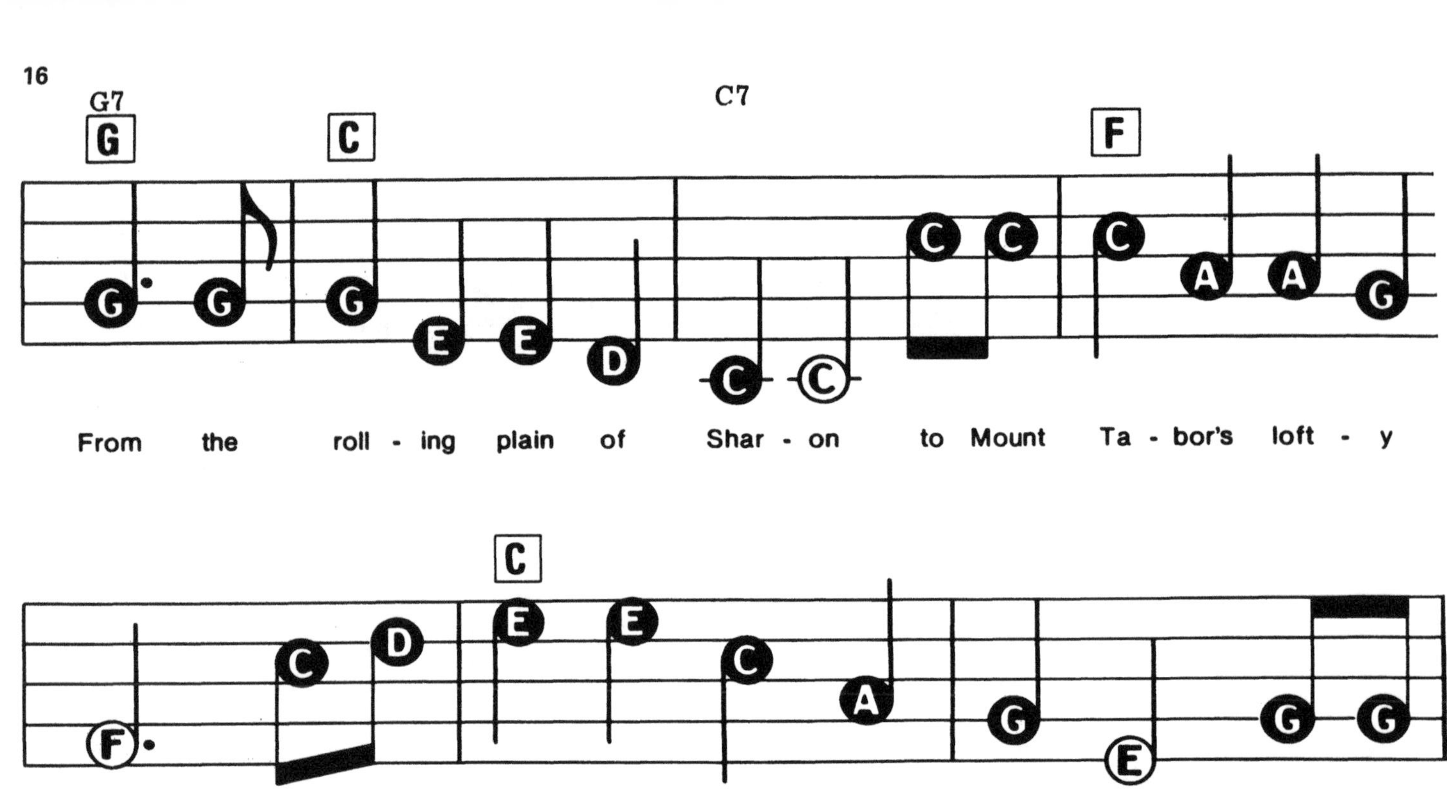
G7 G
C
C7
F
From the roll - ing plain of Shar - on to Mount Ta - bor's loft - y

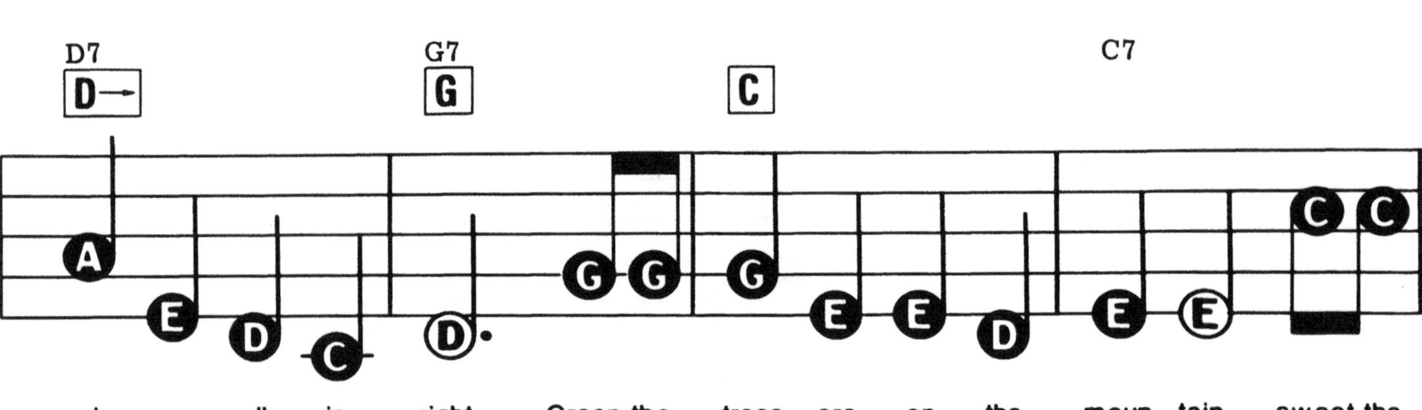
C
heights To the des - ert of Beer - she - ba, all is

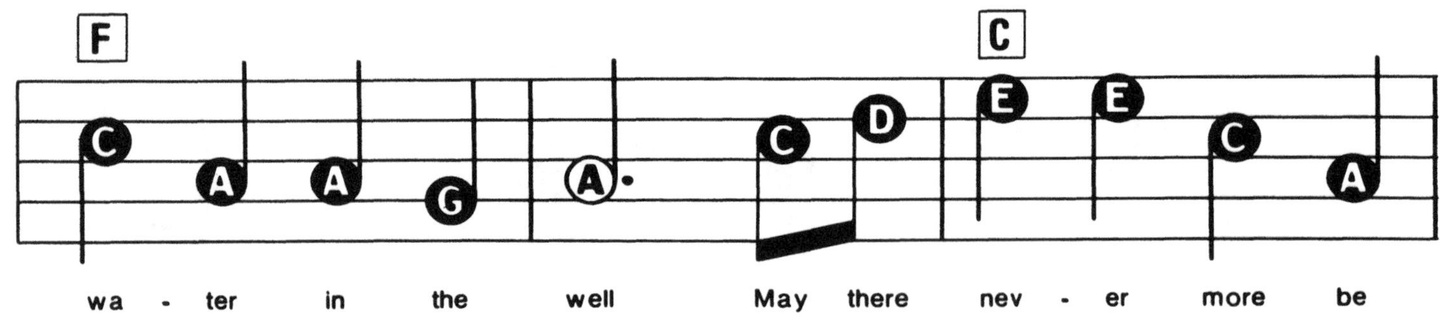
D7 D
G7 G
C
C7
calm; all is right. Green the trees are on the moun - tain, sweet the

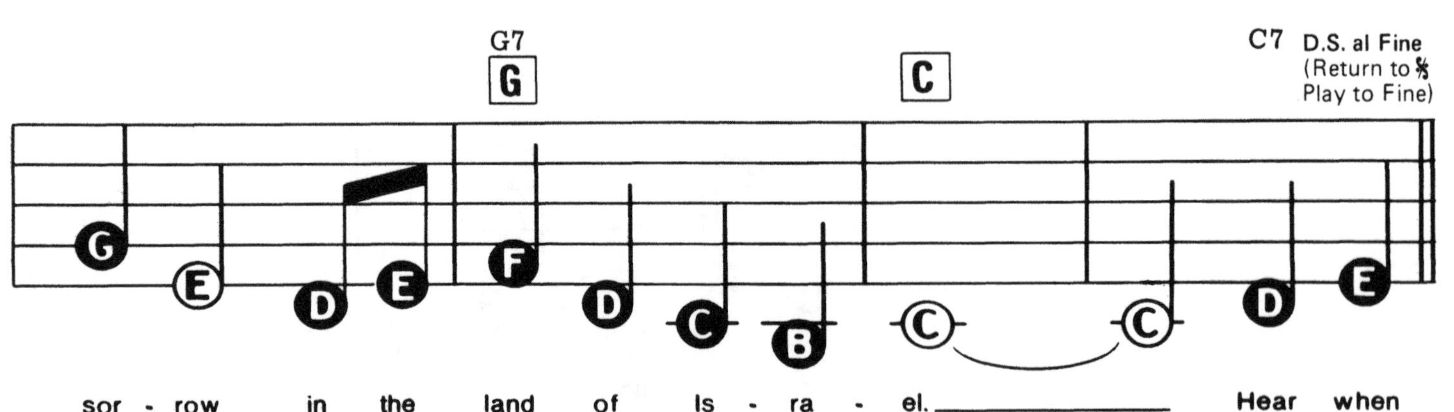
F
C
wa - ter in the well May there nev - er more be
G7 G
C
C7
D.S. al Fine
(Return to 𝄋
Play to Fine)
sor - row in the land of Is - ra - el. Hear when

I'll Fly Away

Registration 6

Words and Music by
Albert E. Brumley

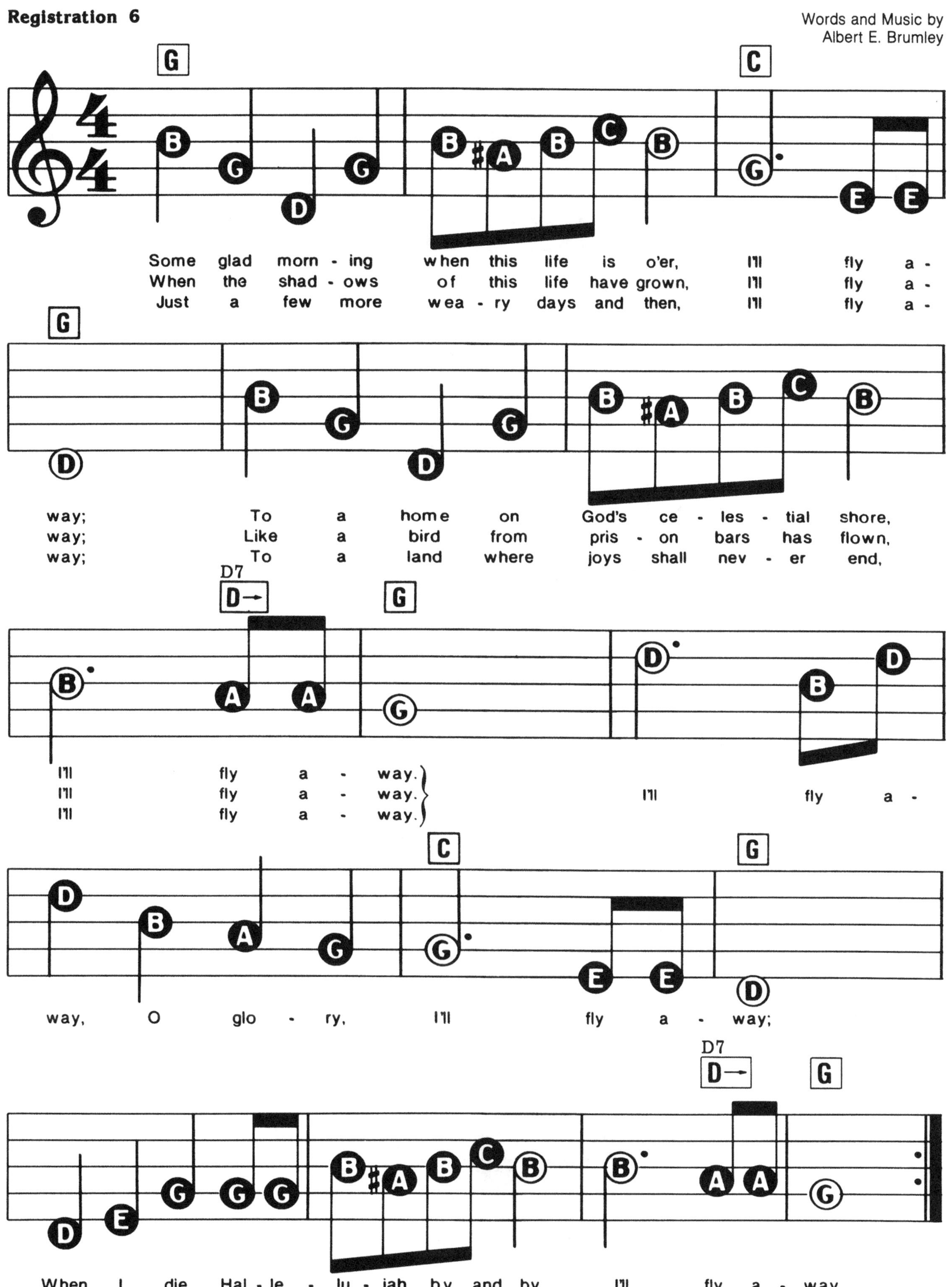

He Turned The Water Into Wine

Registration 7

Words and Music by
Johnny Cash

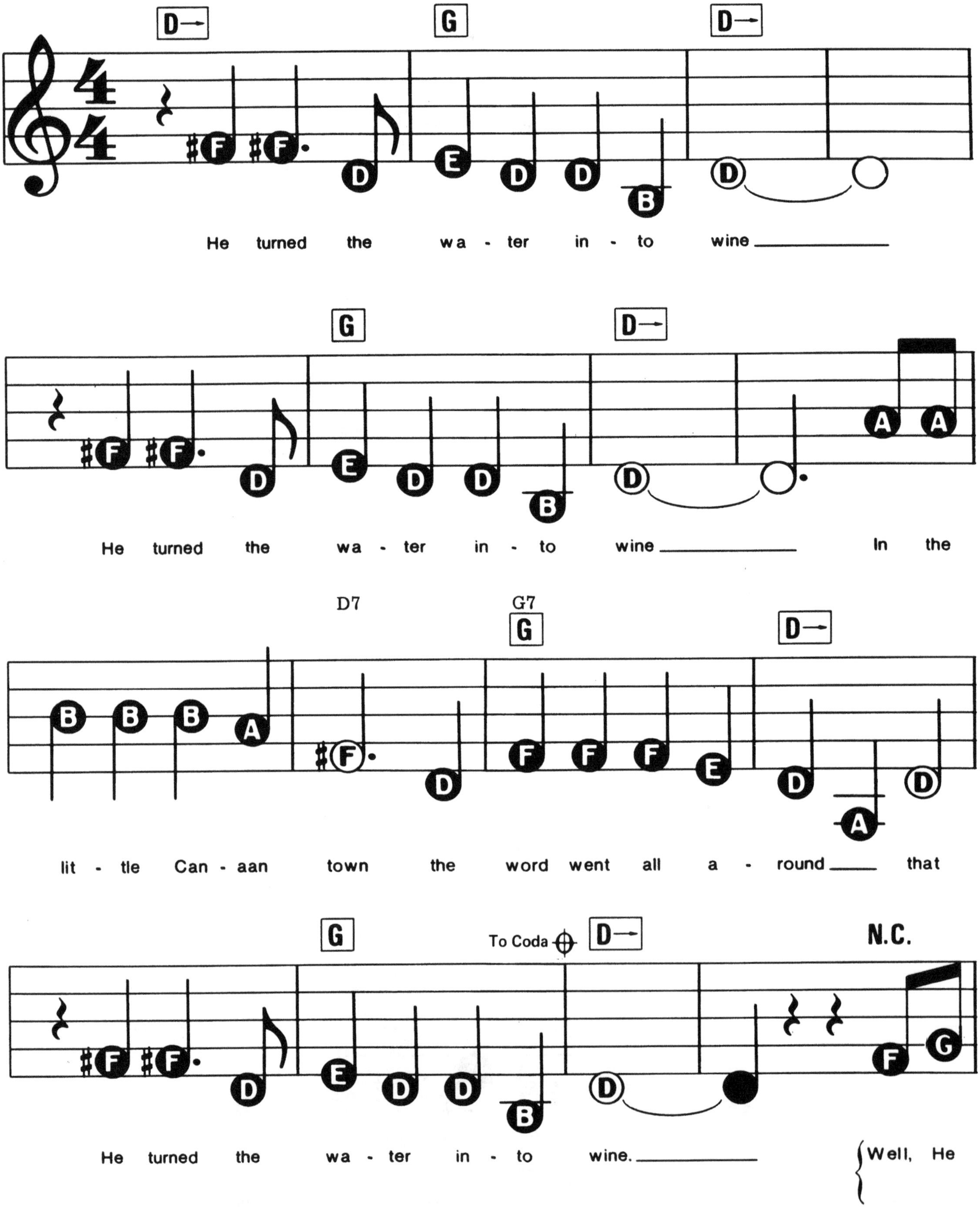

D G D

He turned the wa - ter in - to wine ___

G D

He turned the wa - ter in - to wine ___ In the

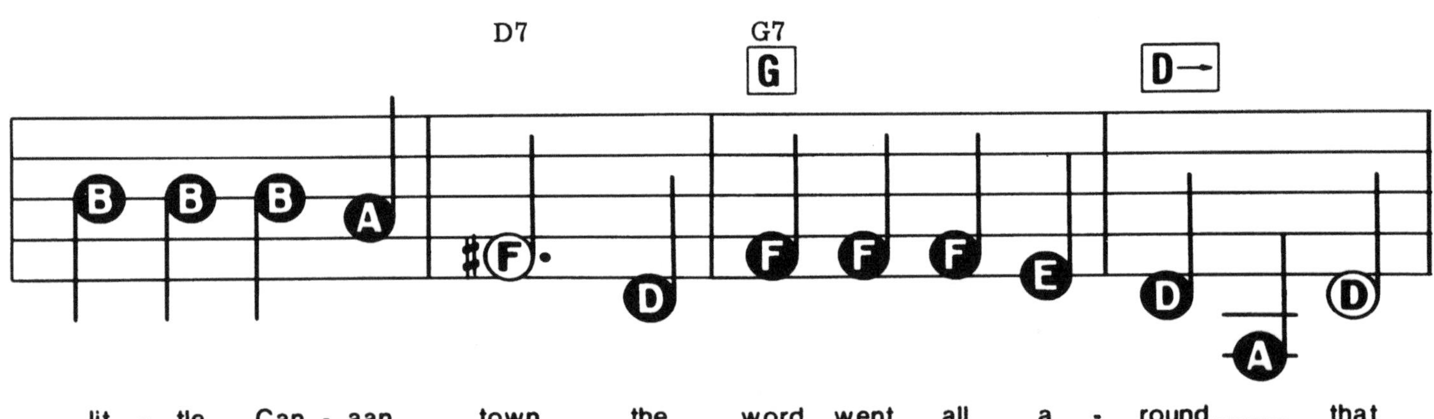

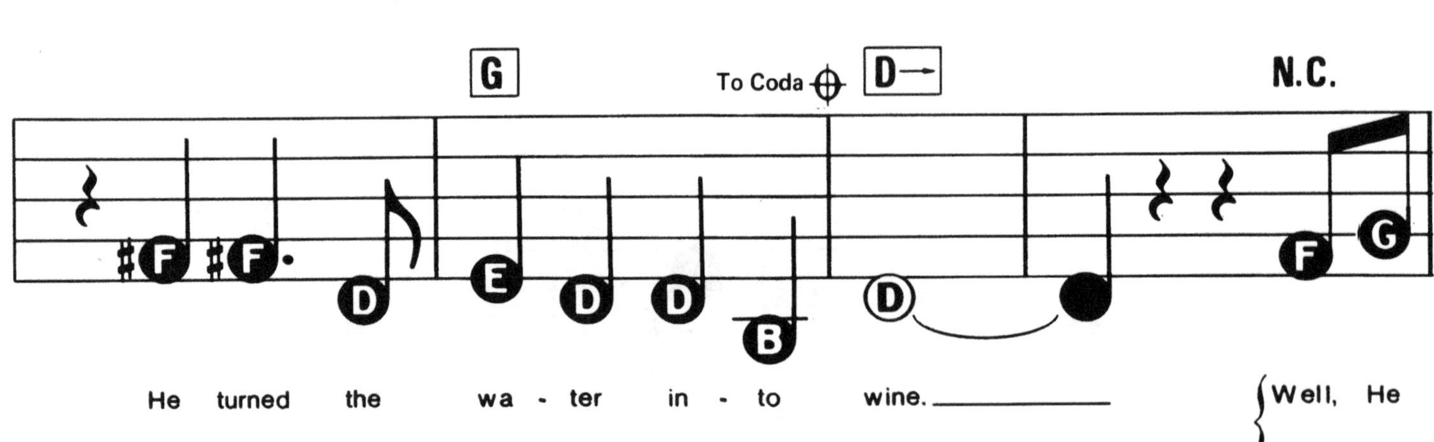

F
Bb
F
walked up - on the Sea of Gal - i - lee He
He healed the le - per and the lame
He fed the hun - gry mul - ti - tude
Bb
F
walked up - on the Sea of Gal - i - lee He
He healed the le - per and the lame He
He fed the hun - gry mul - ti - tude With a
Bb
F
shout - ed far and wide, He calmed the rag - ing tide and
said Go and tell no man, But they shouted it thru the land that
little bit of fish and bread They said ev - 'ry - one was fed
Bb
F
walked up - on the Sea of Gal - i - lee.
He healed the le - per and the lame.
He fed the hun - gry mul - ti - tude.
1,2
D
3
D
D.C. al Coda
(Return to beginning
Play to ⊕ and skip
to Coda)
CODA
D
wine.

The Old Rugged Cross

Registration 2

Words and Music by
Rev. George Bennard

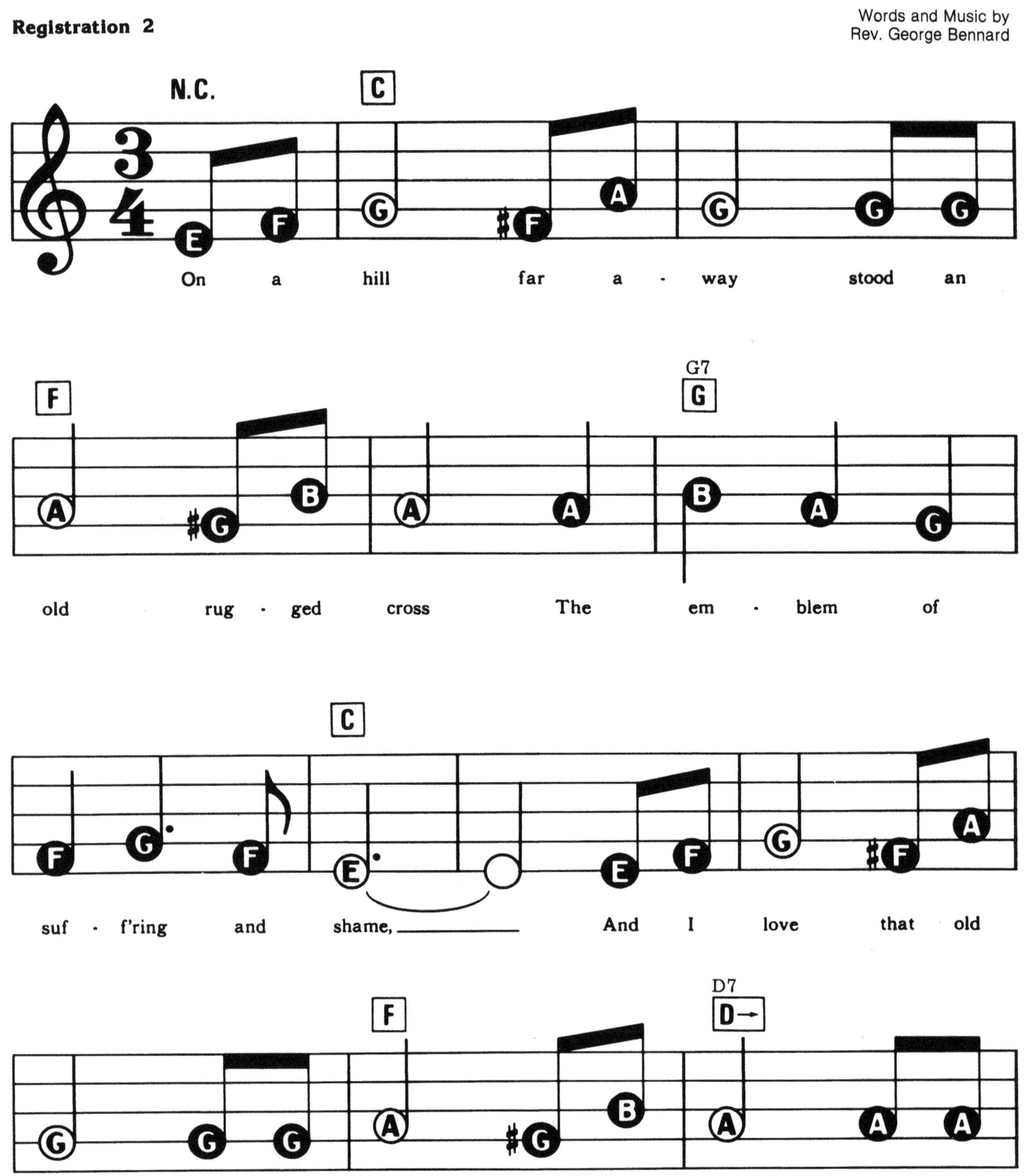

G7
G
C
N.C.
B A G F E D C C B C
world of lost sin - ners was slain. So I'll
Dm
G7
G
C
D D D D C B C C C B
cher - ish the old rug - ged cross, Till my
F
C
A A A C B A G G G C
tro - phies at last I lay down, I will
A7
A
Dm
E E E E F E A A F F
cling to the old rug - ged cross, And ex-
C
G7
G
C
E D C G B D C C
change it some day for a crown.

Lead Me, Father

Registration 10

Words and Music by
Johnny Cash

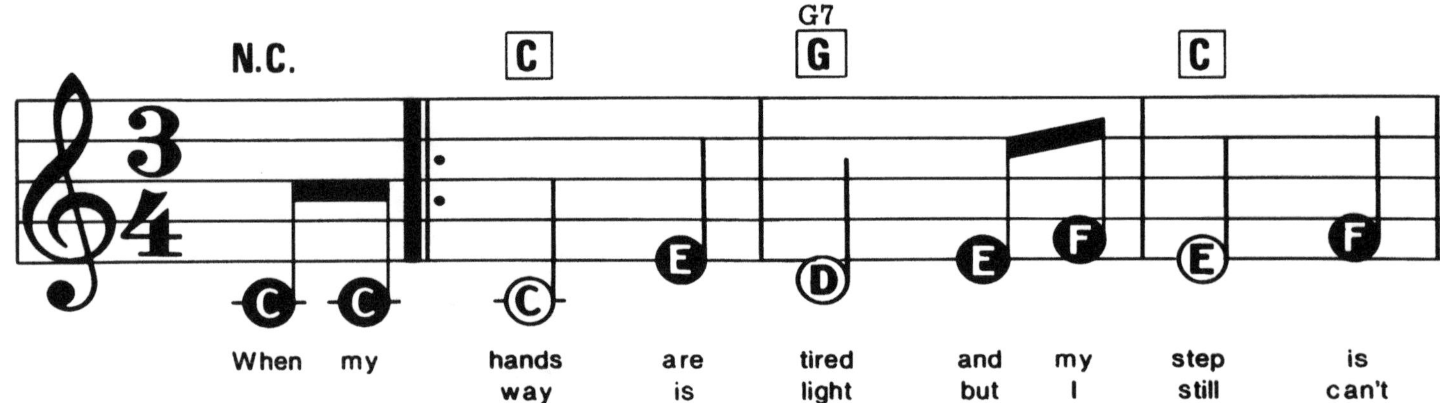

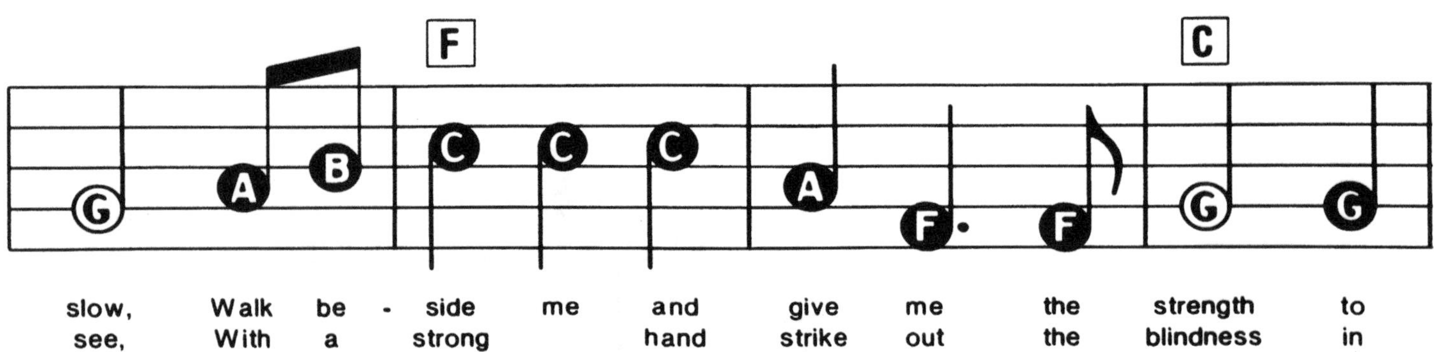

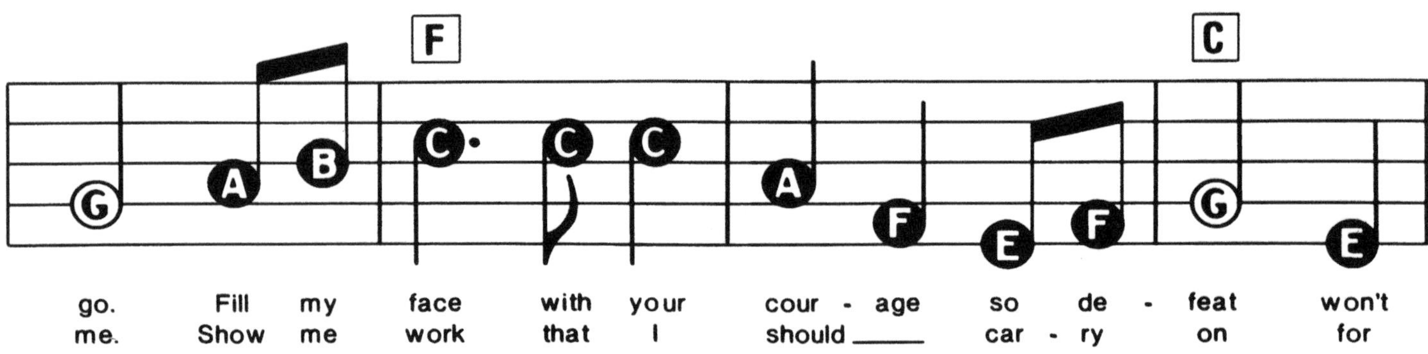

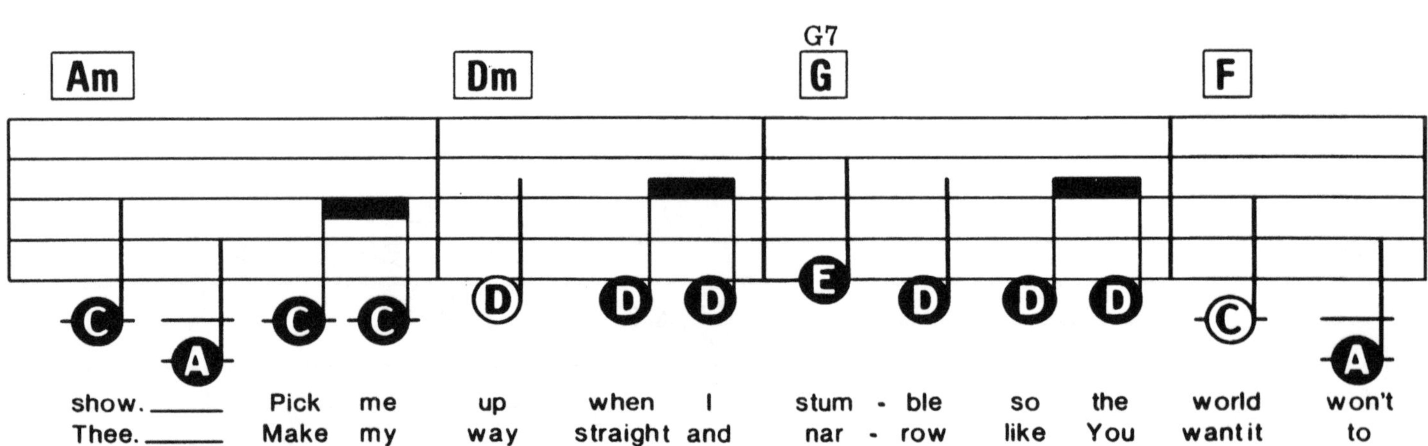

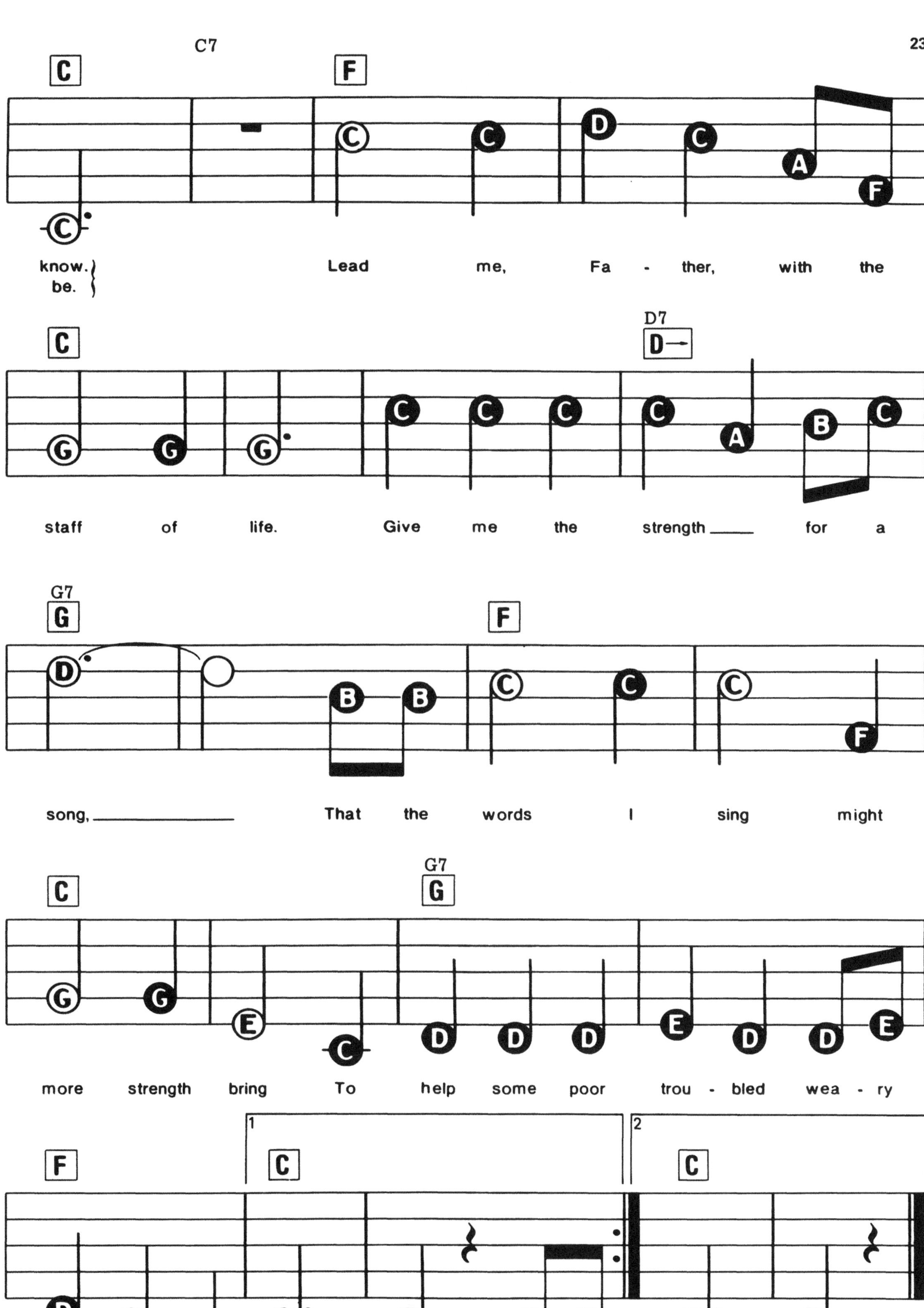
C7
know.
be.
Lead me, Fa - ther, with the
D7
staff of life. Give me the strength for a
G7
song, That the words I sing might
G7
more strength bring To help some poor trou - bled wea - ry
1
2
work - er a - long. When my long.

These Hands

Registration 4

Words and Music by
Eddie Noack

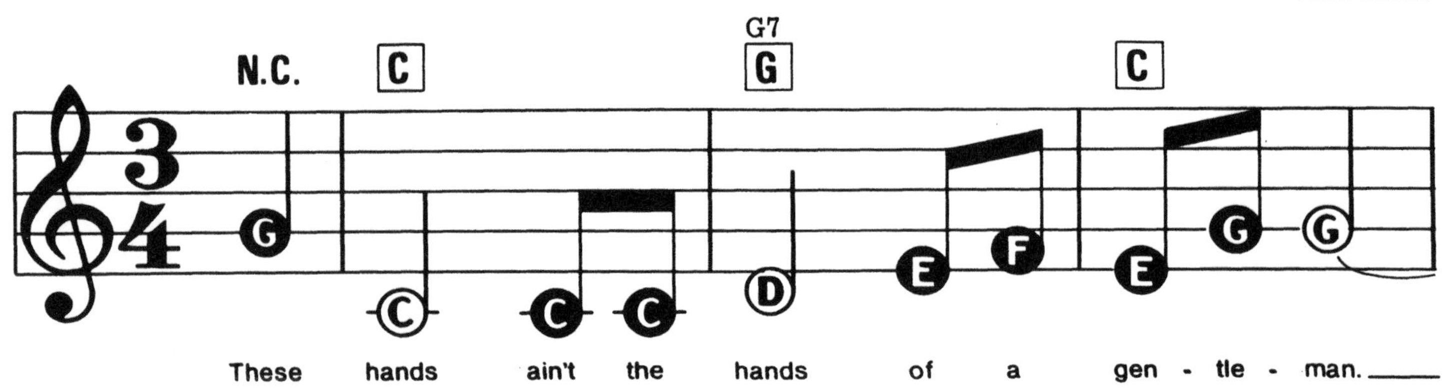

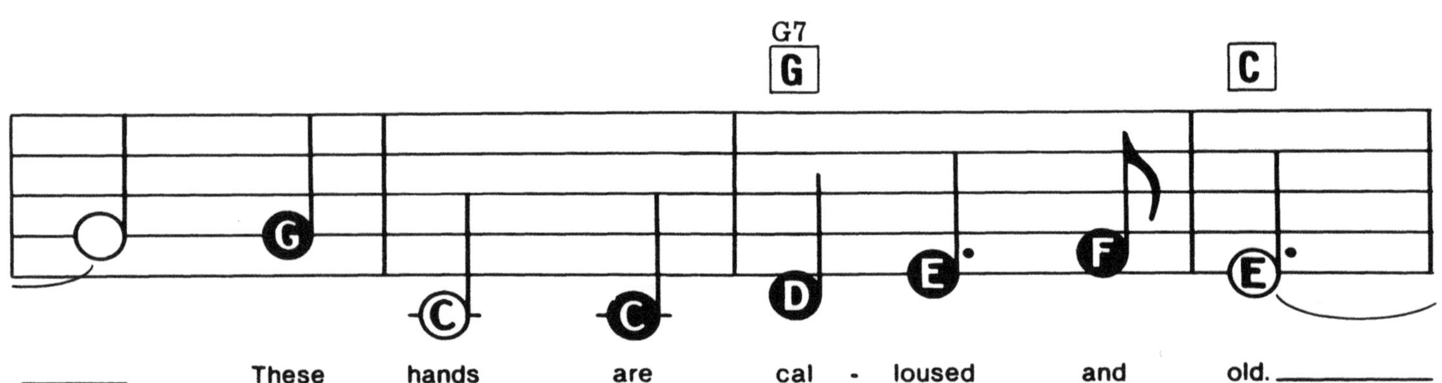

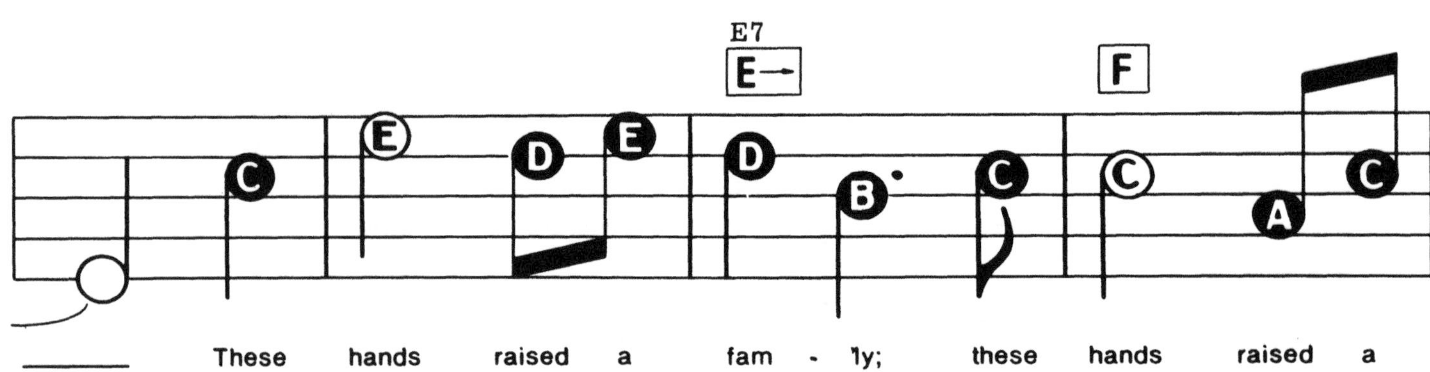

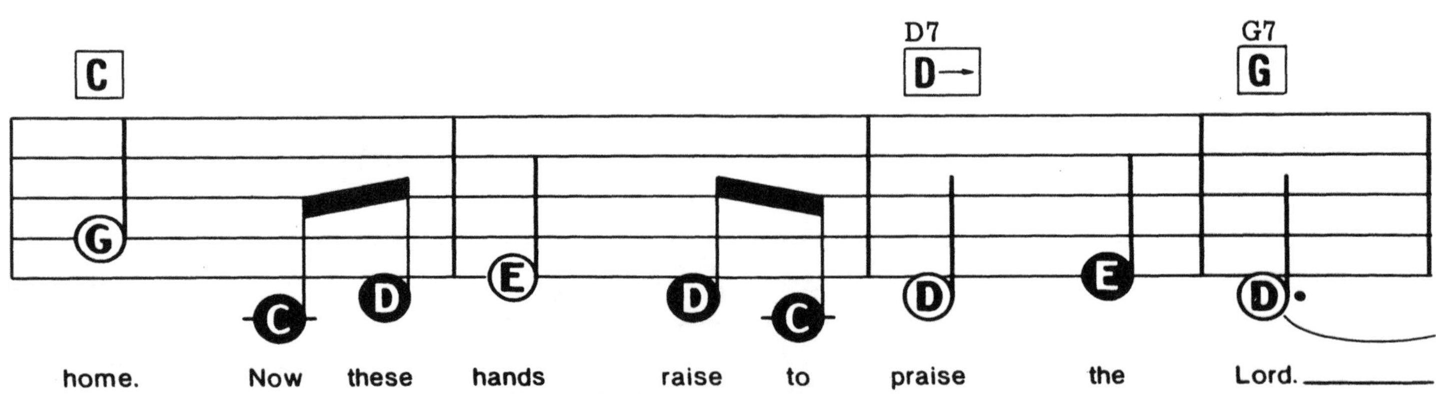

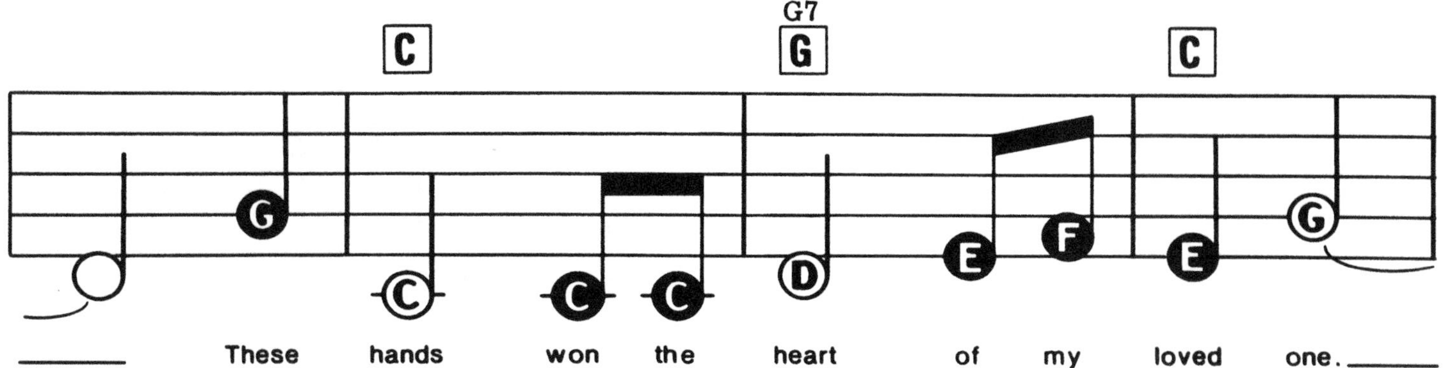
C
G7
G
C
G
C
C
C
D
E
F
E
G
These hands won the heart of my loved one.

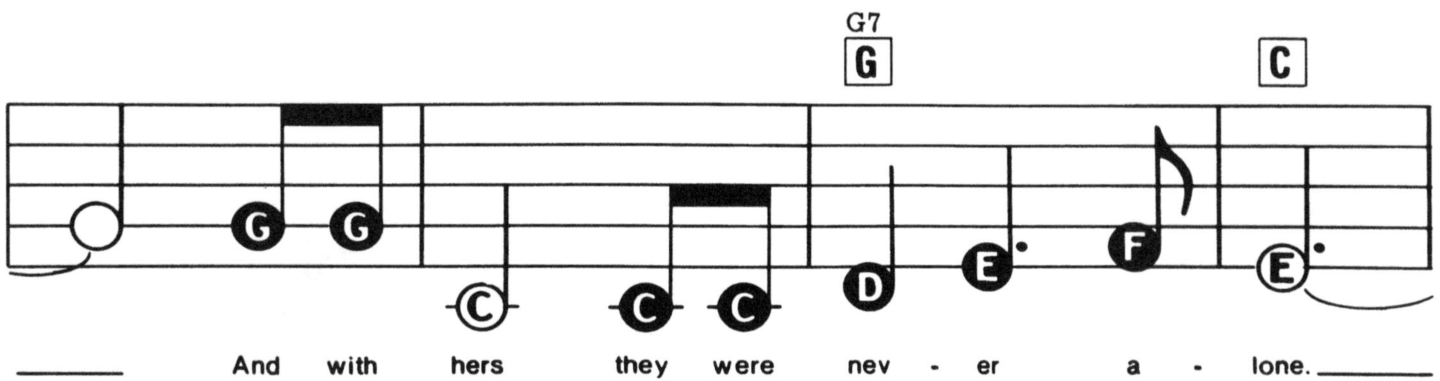
G7
G
C
G
G
C
C
C
D
E
F
E
And with hers they were nev - er a - lone.

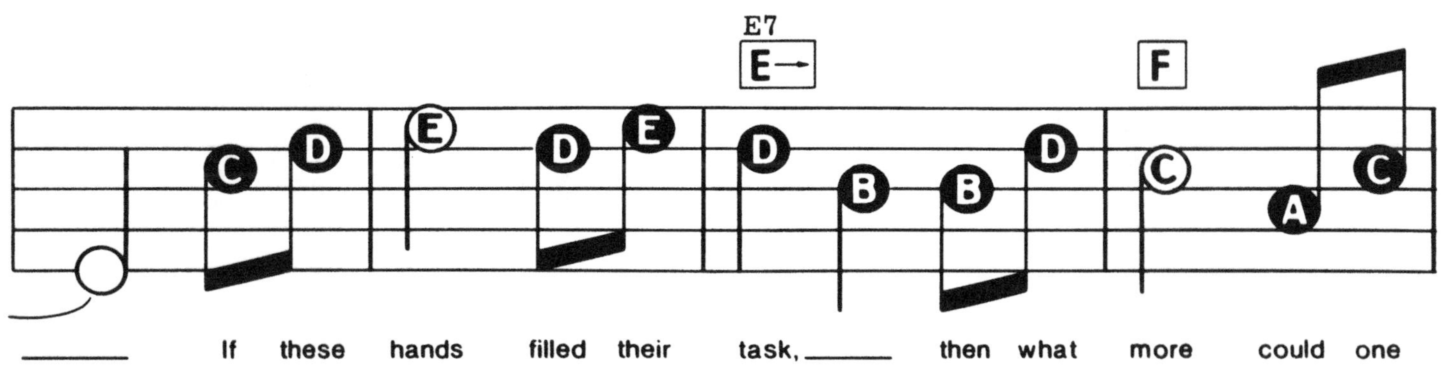
E7
E
F
C
D
E
D
E
D
B
B
D
C
A
C
If these hands filled their task, then what more could one

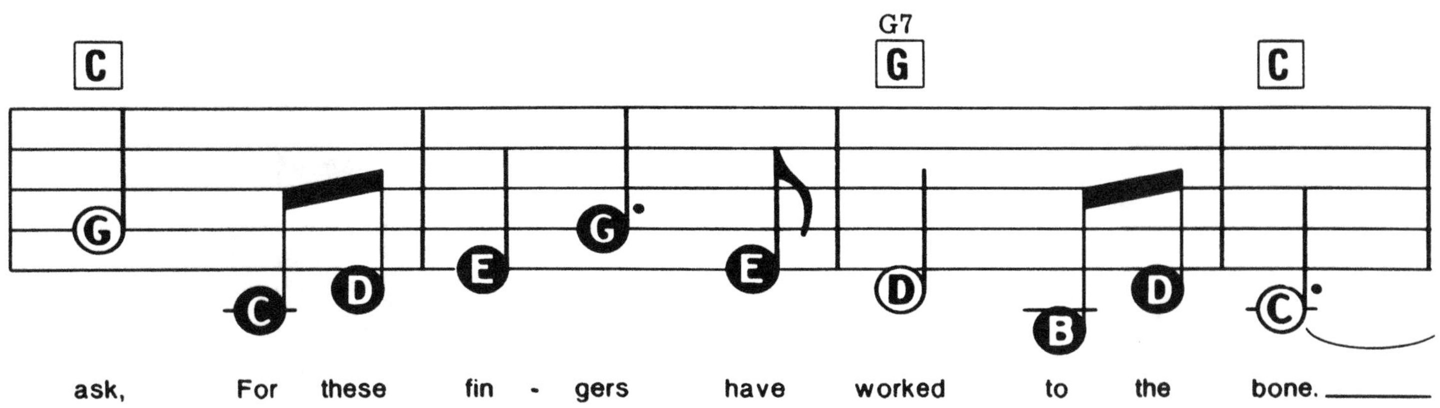
C
G7
G
C
G
C
D
E
G
E
D
B
D
C
ask, For these fin - gers have worked to the bone.

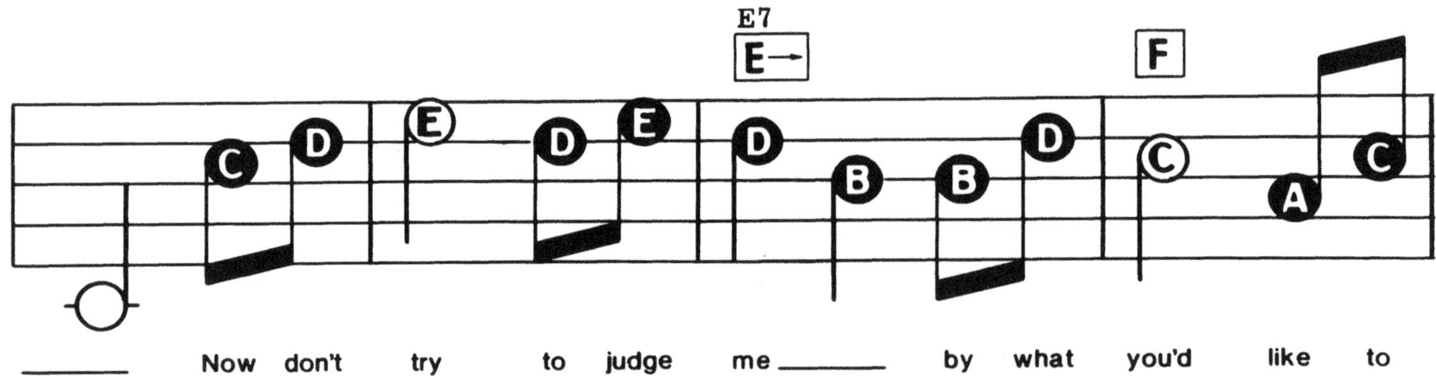
E7
E
F
C D E D E D B B D C A C
Now don't try to judge me by what you'd like to

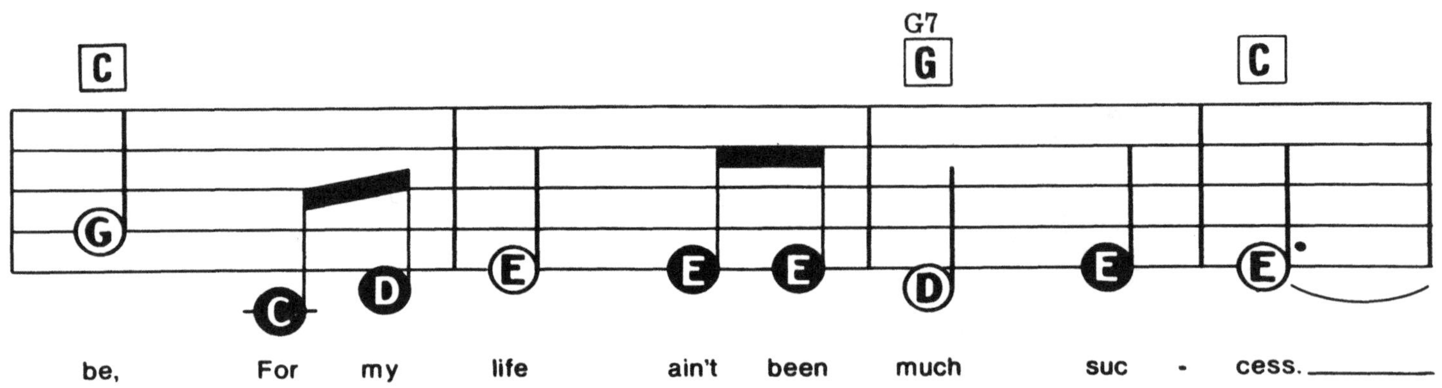
C
G7
G
C
G C D E E E D E E
be, For my life ain't been much suc - cess.

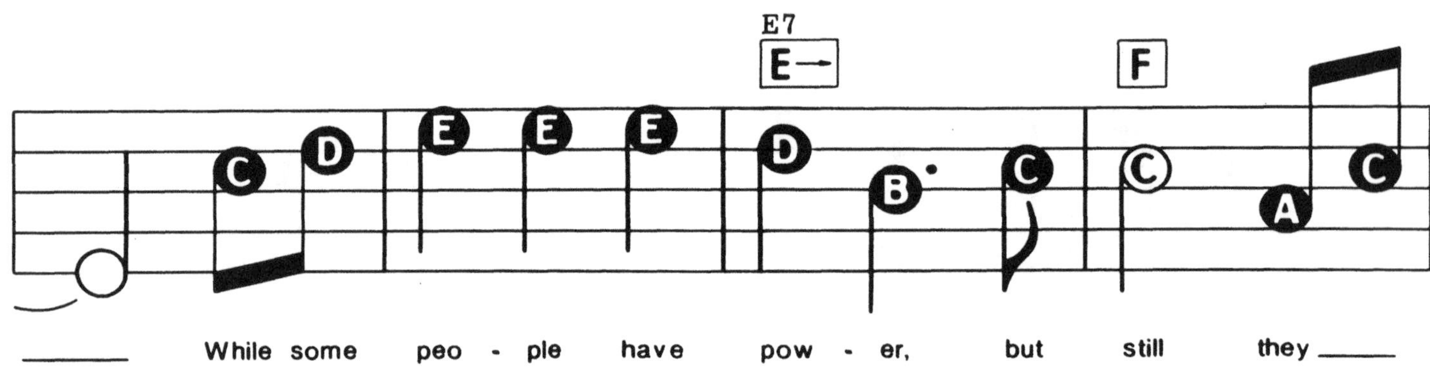
E7
E
F
C D E E E D B C C A C
While some peo - ple have pow - er, but still they

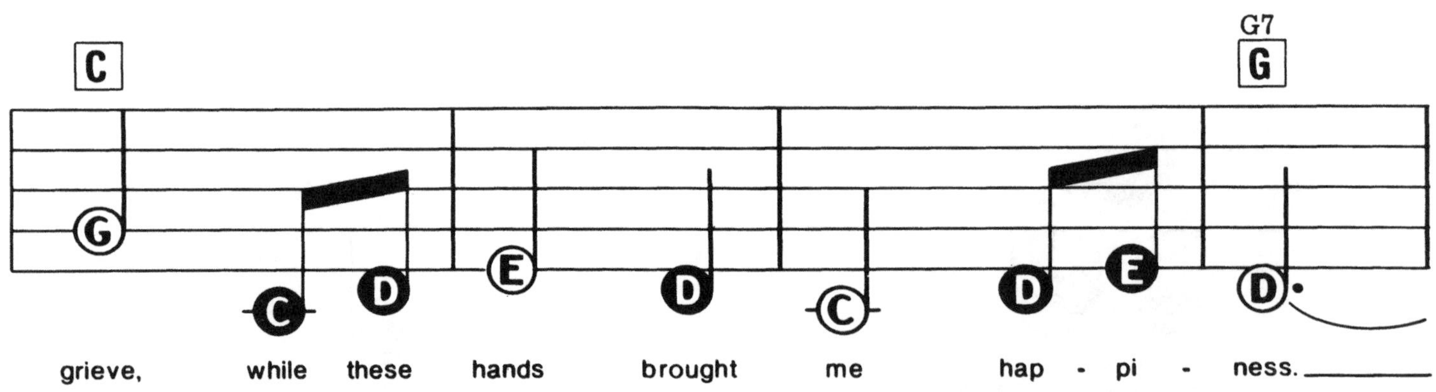
C
G7
G
G C D E D C D E D
grieve, while these hands brought me hap - pi - ness.

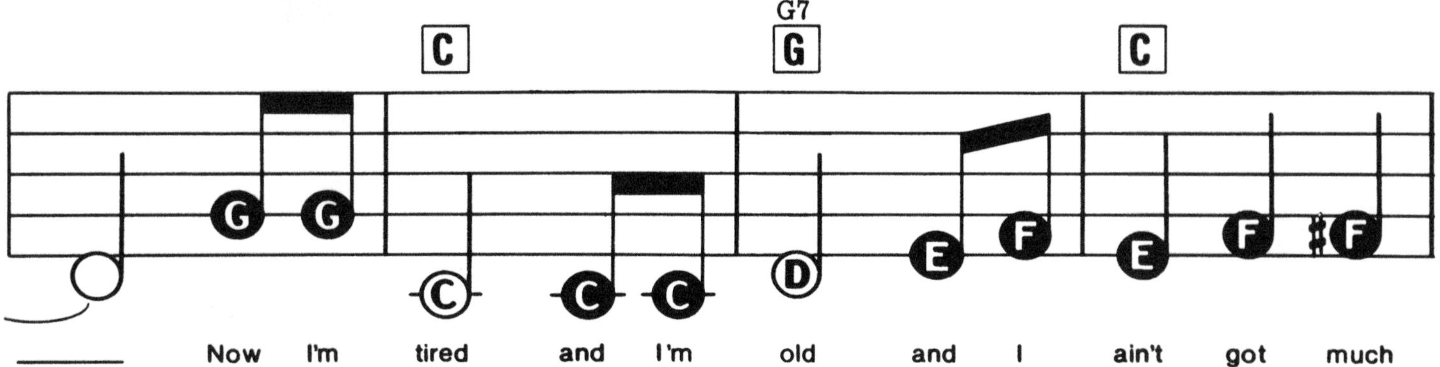
C
G7
G
C
G G C C C D E F E F #F
Now I'm tired and I'm old and I ain't got much

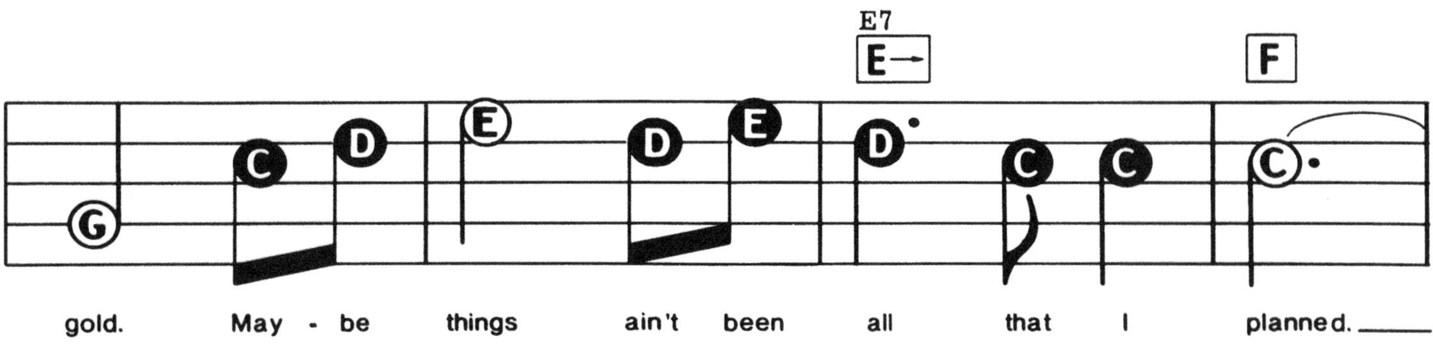
E7
E
F
G C D E D E D C C C
gold. May - be things ain't been all that I planned.

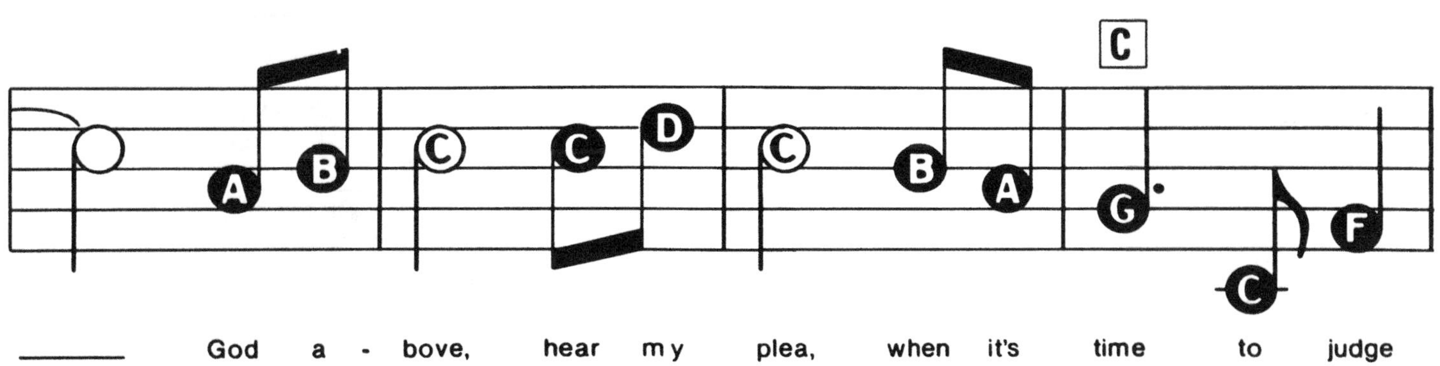
C
A B C C D C B A G C F
God a - bove, hear my plea, when it's time to judge

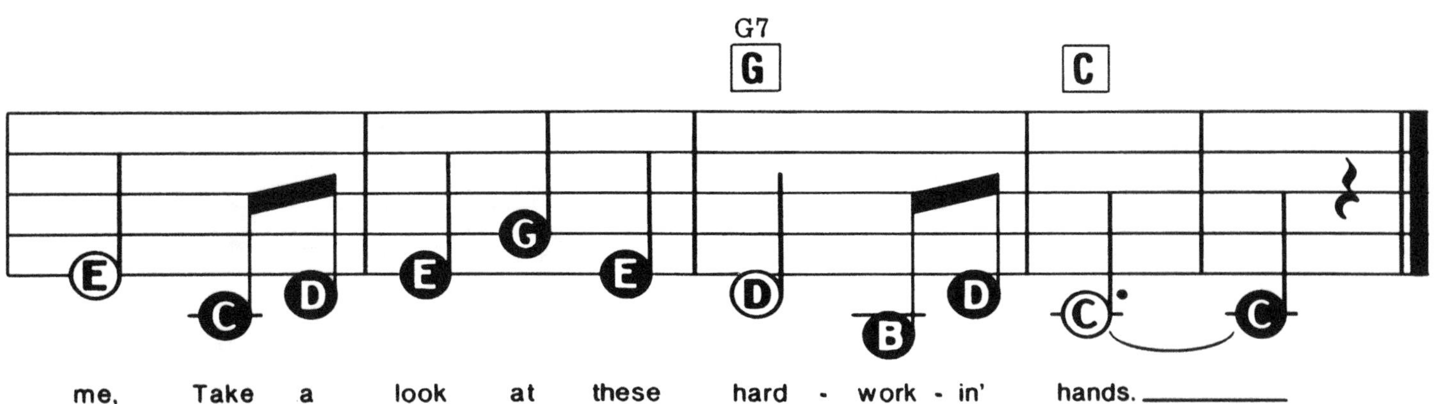
G7
G
C
E C D E G E D B D C C
me, Take a look at these hard - work - in' hands.

The Great Speckled Bird

Registration 1

Words and Music by
Johnny Cash

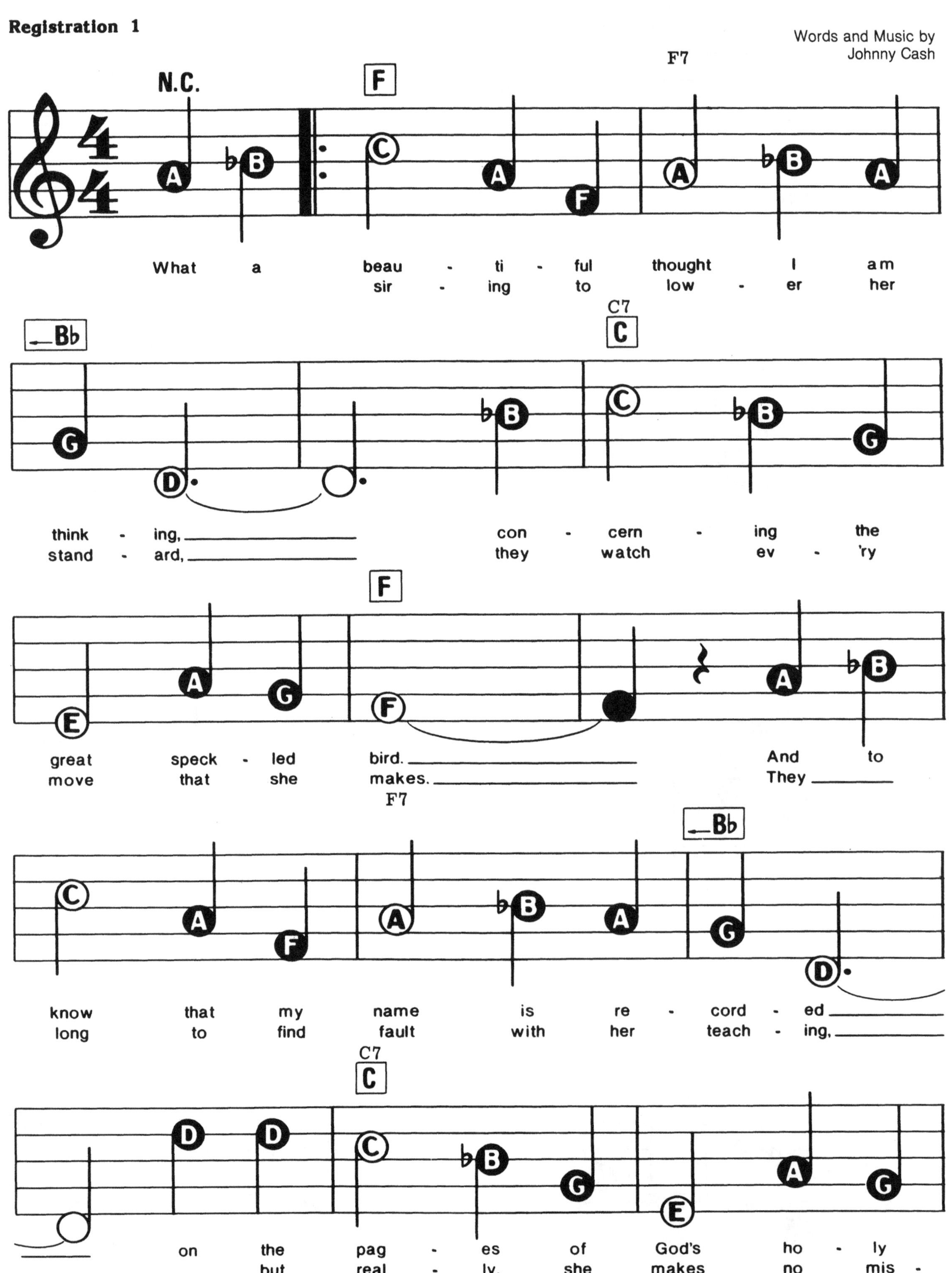

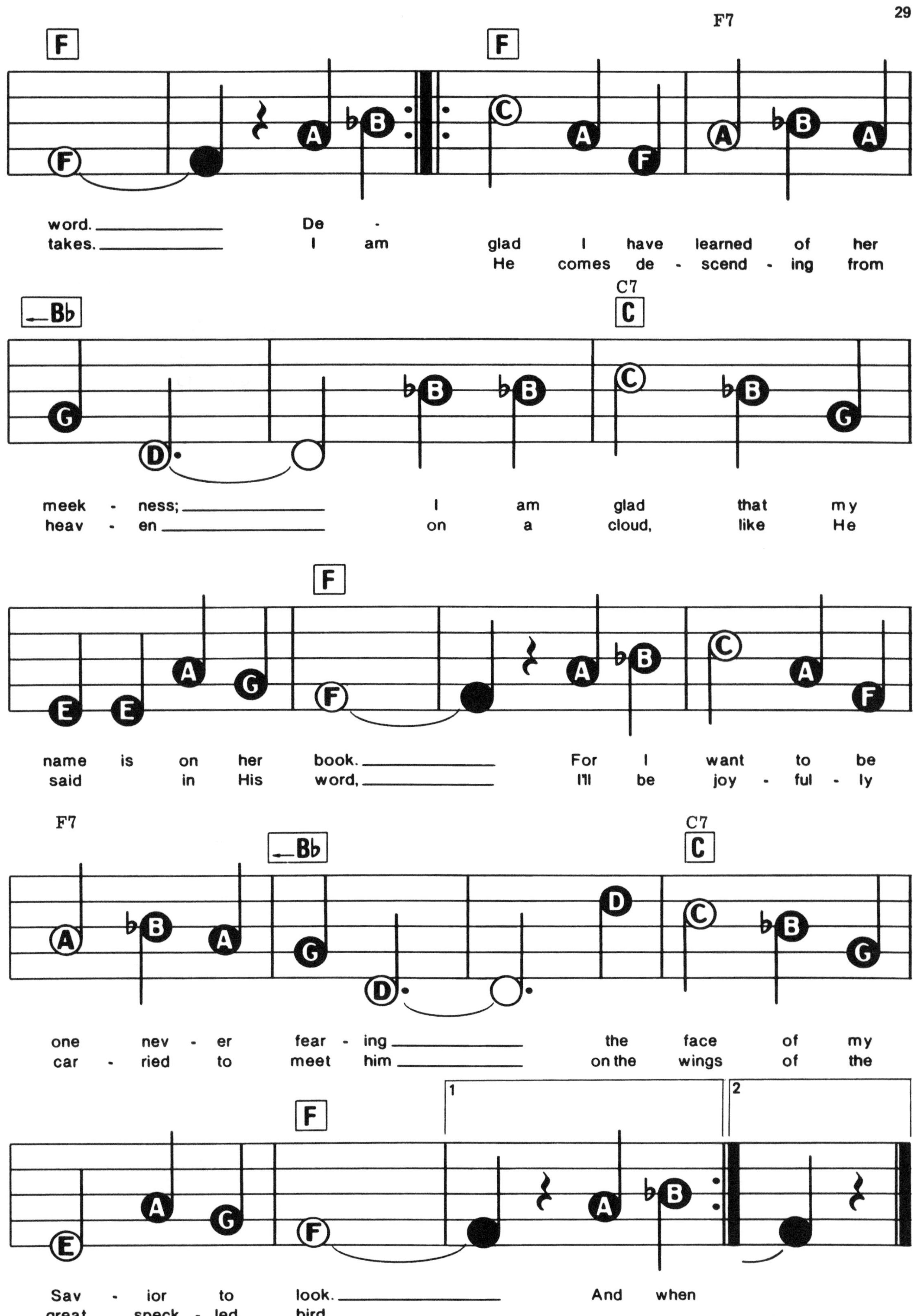
F
F7
F
word. De -
takes. I am glad I have learned of her
He comes de - scend - ing from
Bb
C7
C
meek - ness; I am glad that my
heav - en on a cloud, like He
F
name is on her book. For I want to be
said in His word, I'll be joy - ful - ly
F7
Bb
C7
C
one nev - er fear - ing the face of my
car - ried to meet him on the wings of the
F
1
2
Sav - ior to look. And when
great speck - led bird.

Wings In The Morning

Registration 1

Words and Music by
Johnny Cash

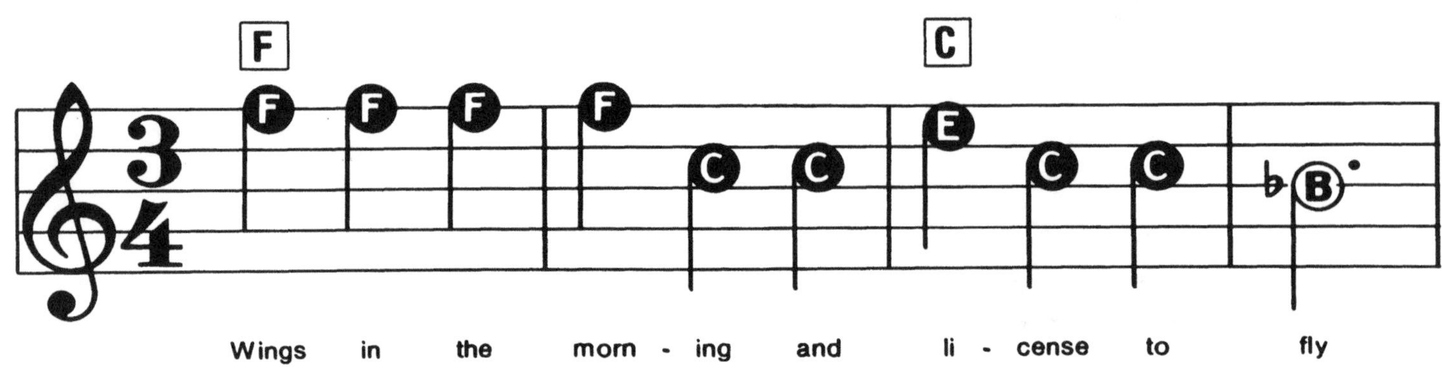

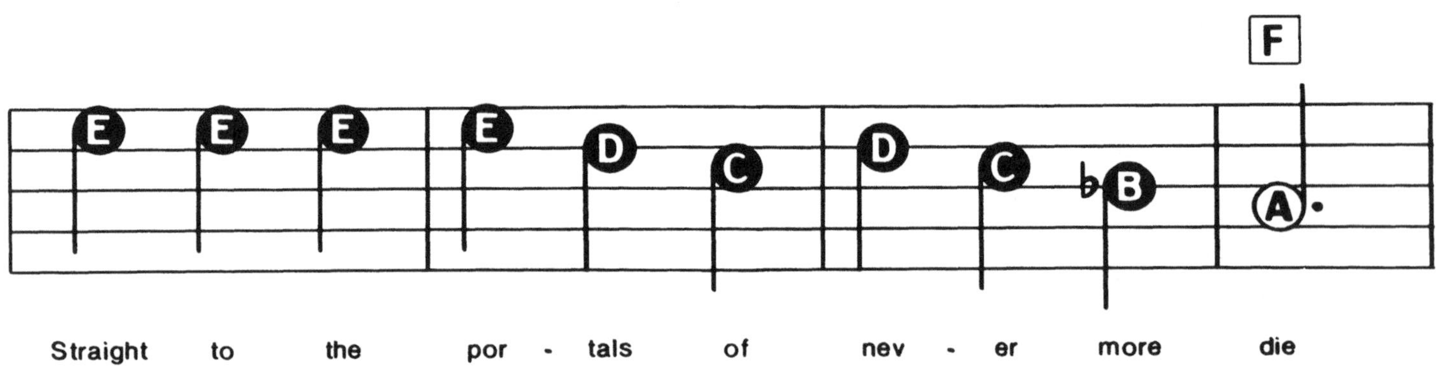

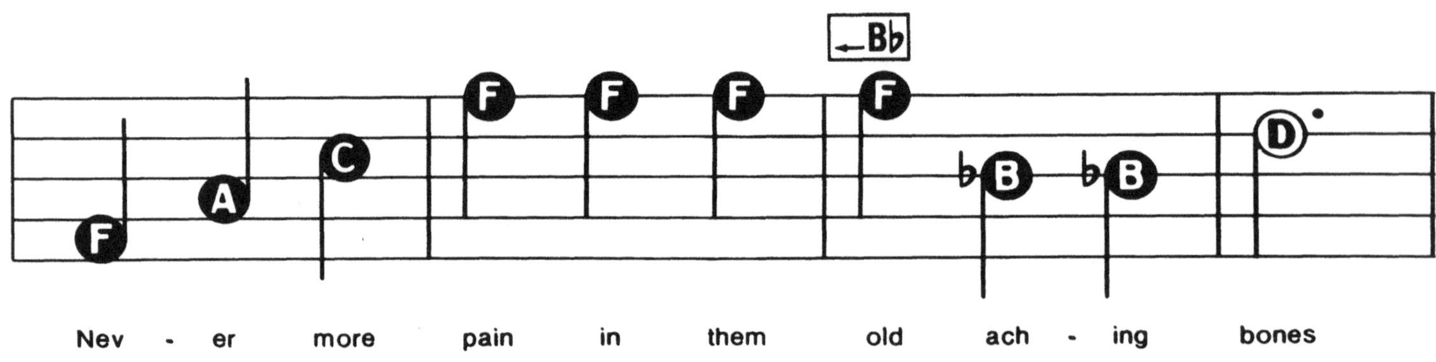

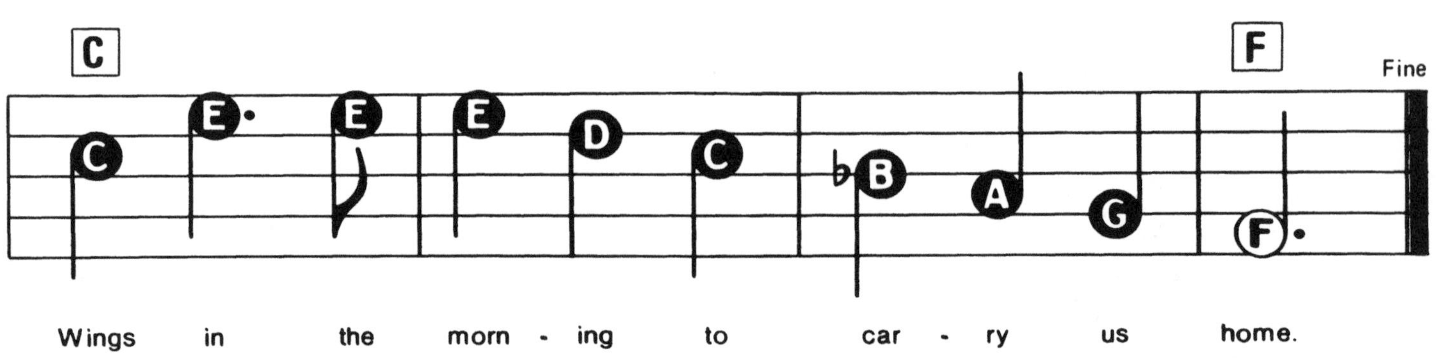

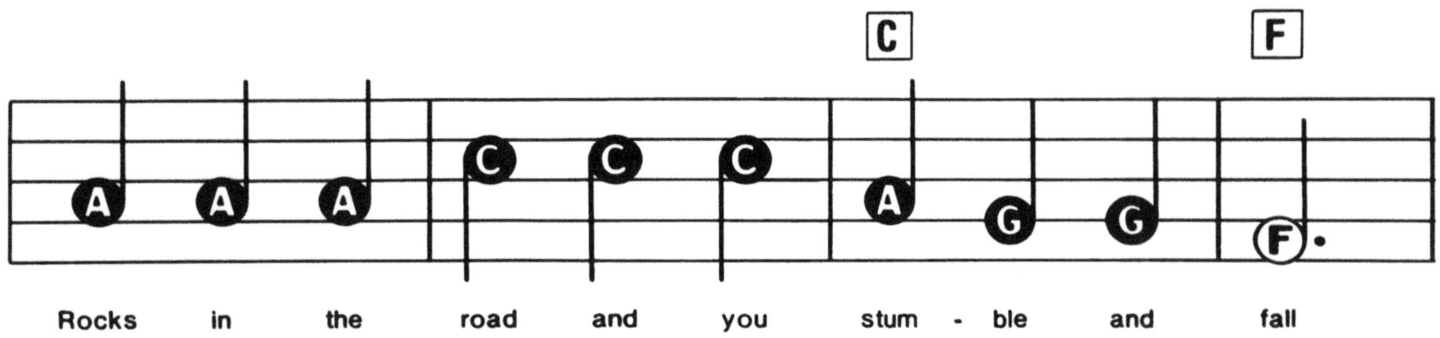
C
F
A A A C C C A G G F
Rocks in the road and you stum - ble and fall

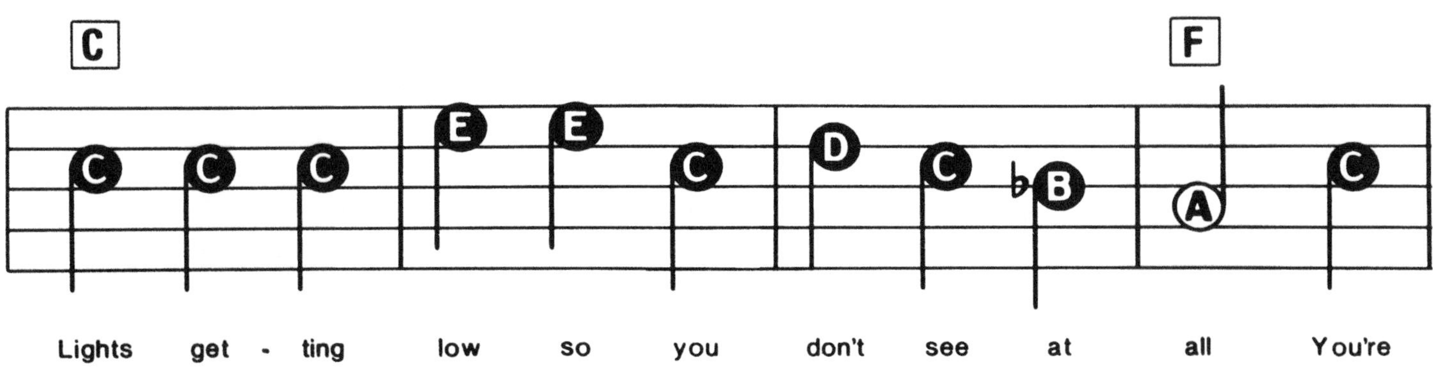
C
F
C C C E E C D C ♭B A C
Lights get - ting low so you don't see at all You're

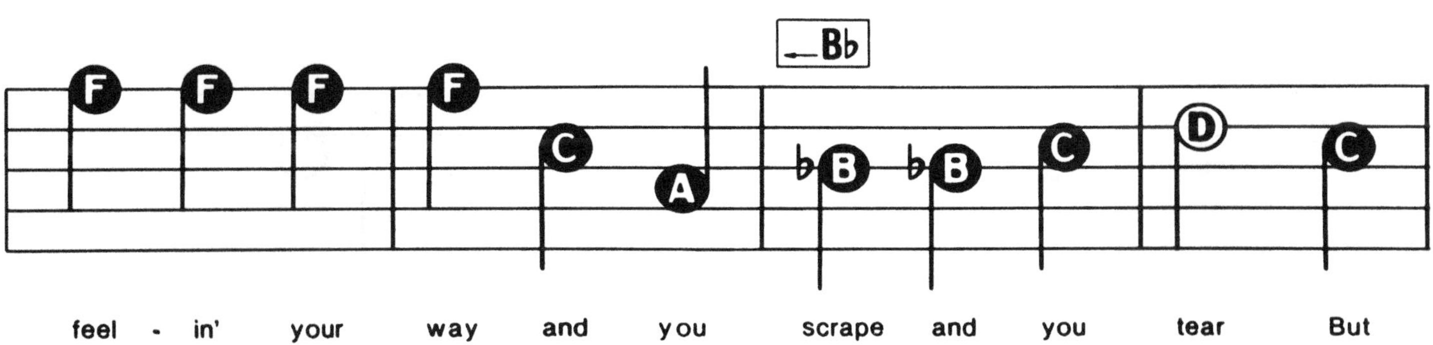
Bb
F F F F C A ♭B ♭B C D C
feel - in' your way and you scrape and you tear But

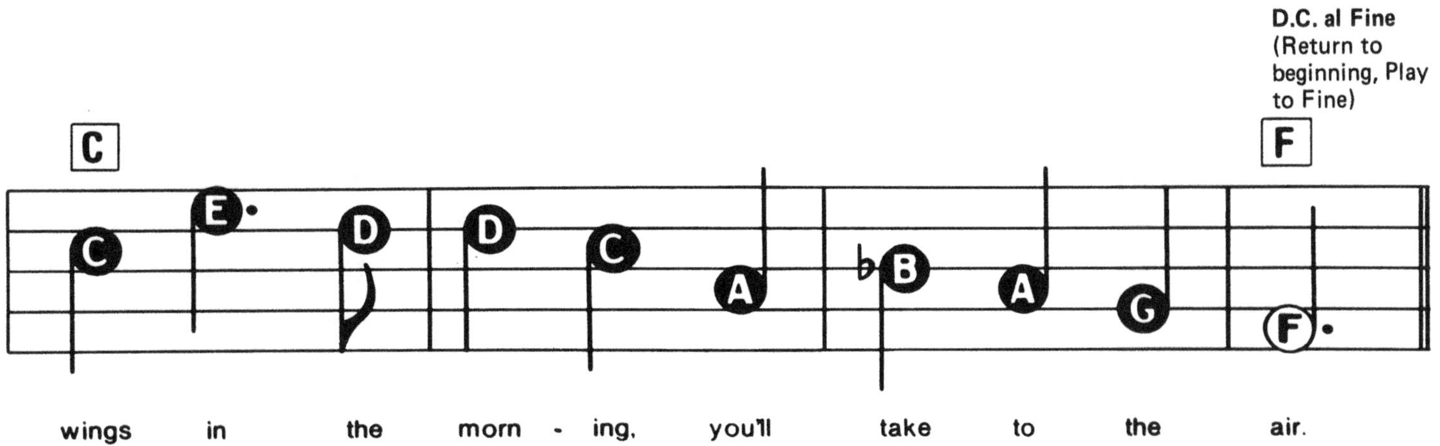
D.C. al Fine
(Return to
beginning, Play
to Fine)
C
F
C E D D C A ♭B A G F
wings in the morn - ing, you'll take to the air.

Were You There

Registration 2

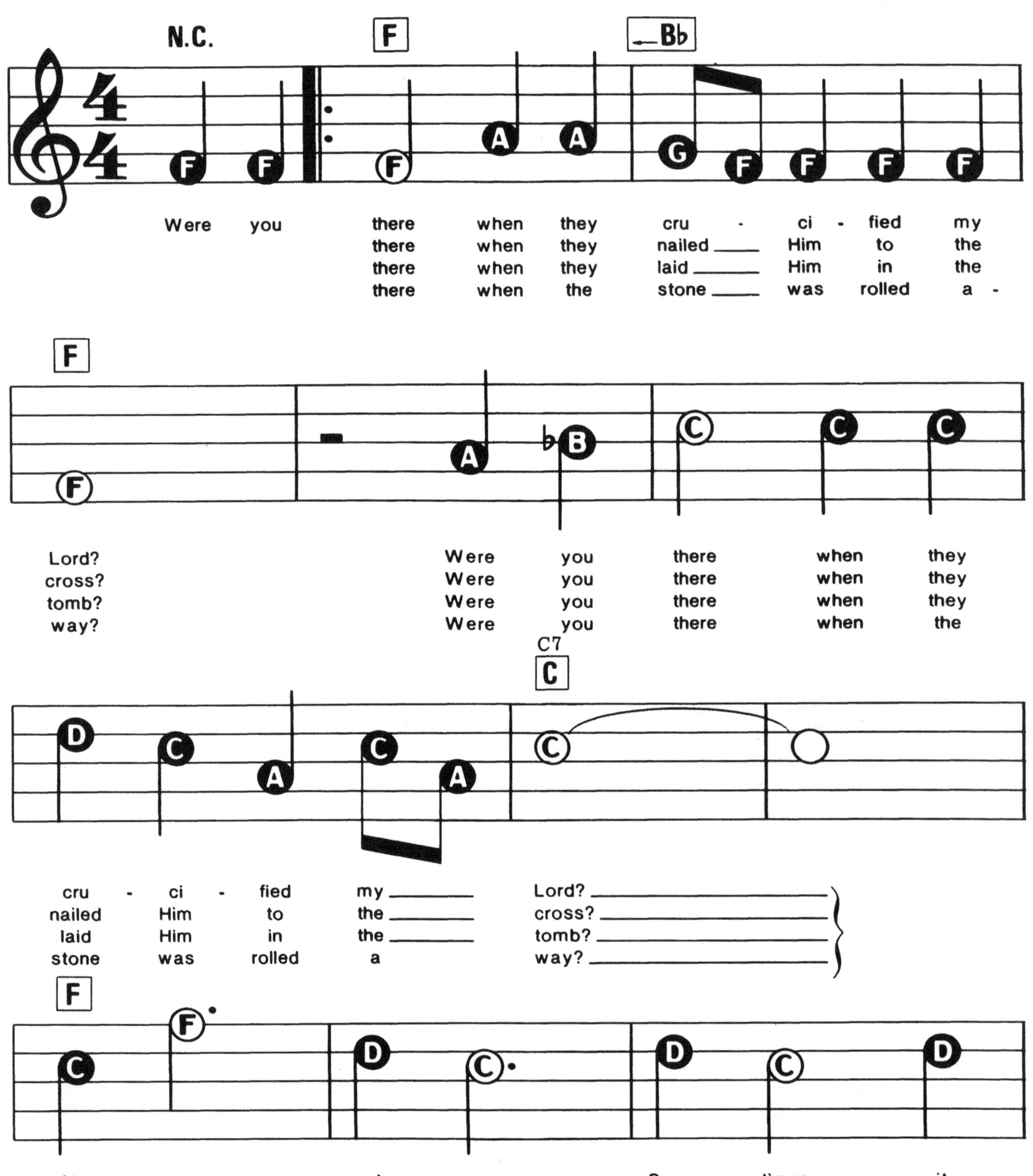

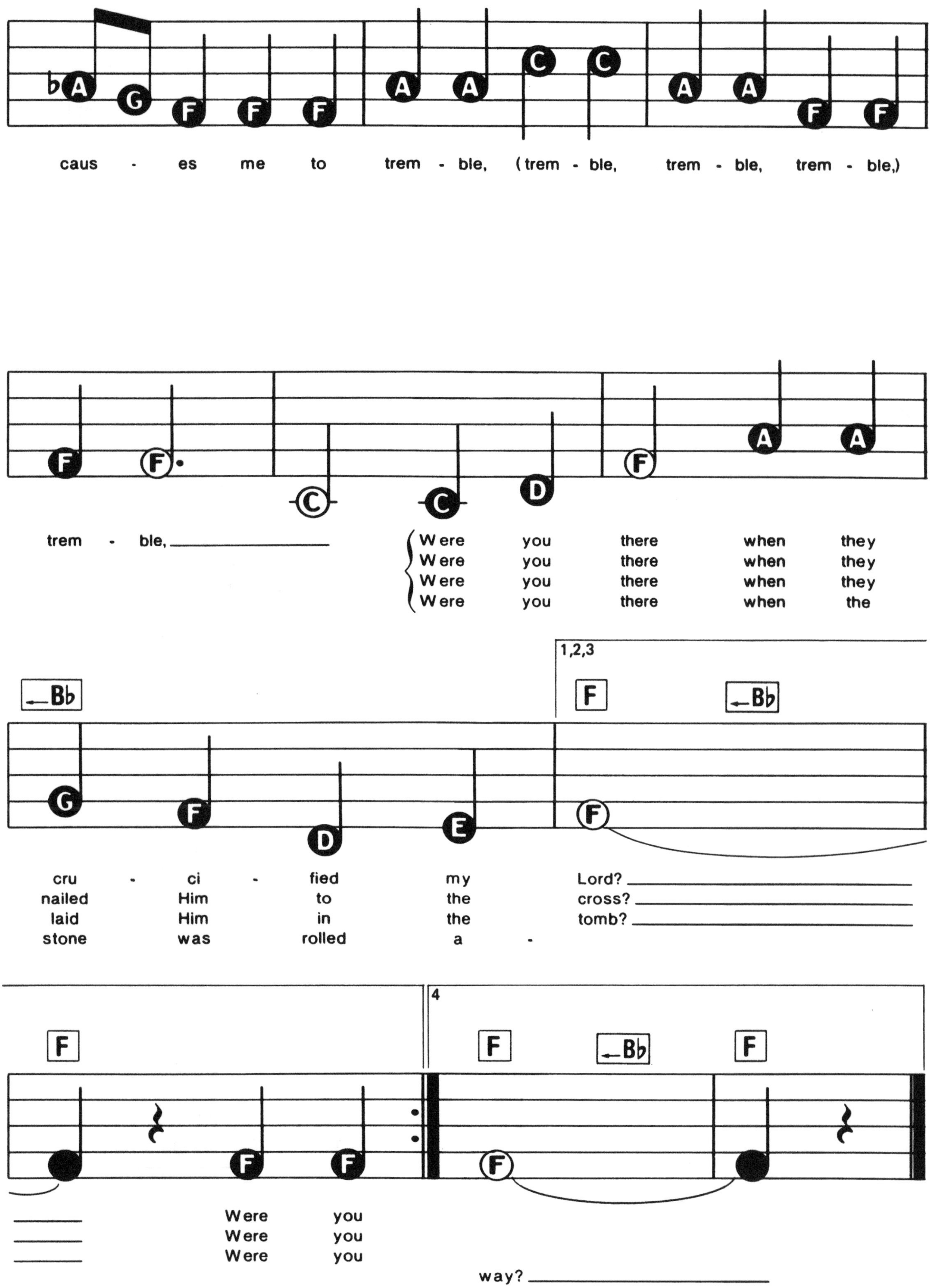

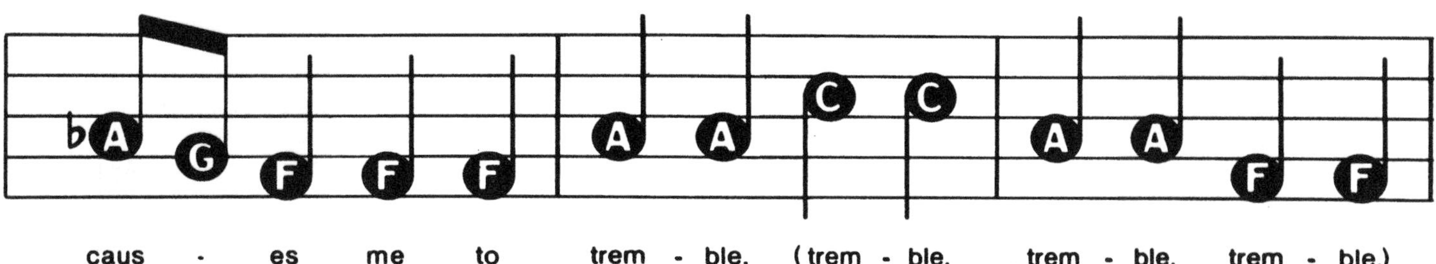

trem - ble, ___

Were you there when they cru - ci - fied my Lord? ___ Were you
Were you there when they nailed Him to the cross? ___ Were you
Were you there when they laid Him in the tomb? ___ Were you
Were you there when the stone was rolled a - way? ___

B♭ F B♭ F

1,2,3

4

F B♭ F

It Was Jesus

Registration 8

Words and Music by
Johnny Cash

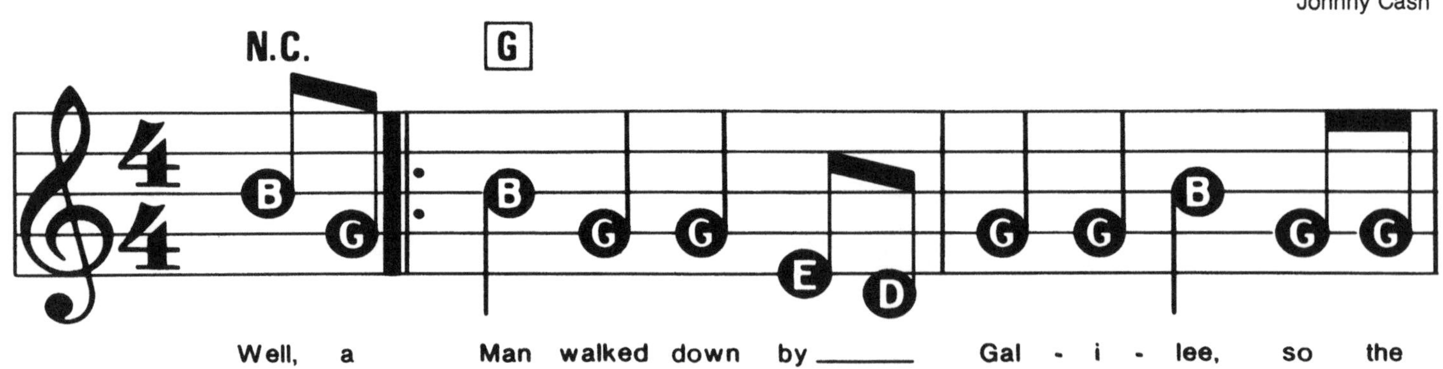

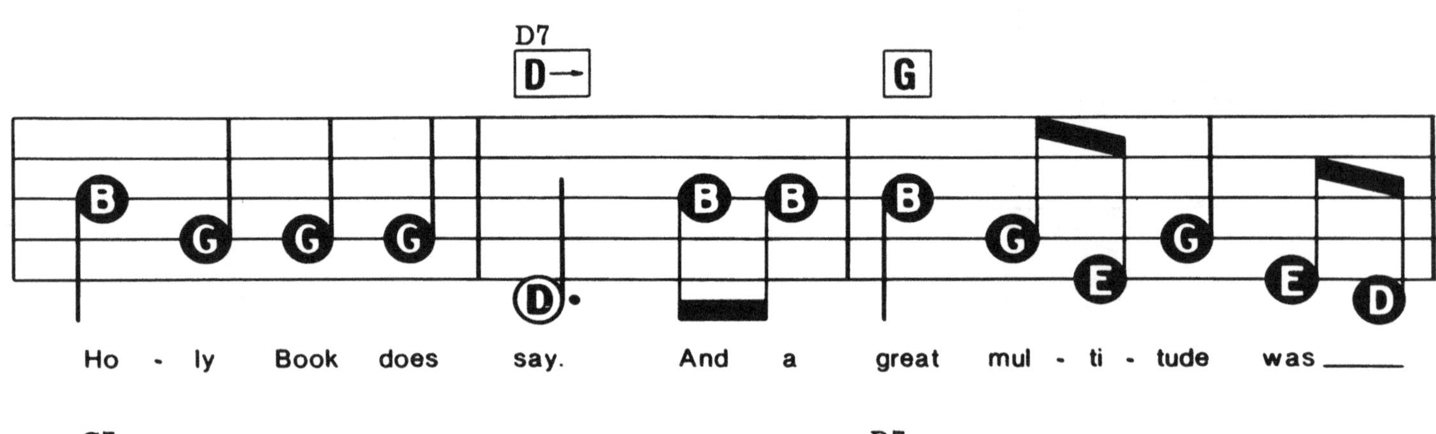

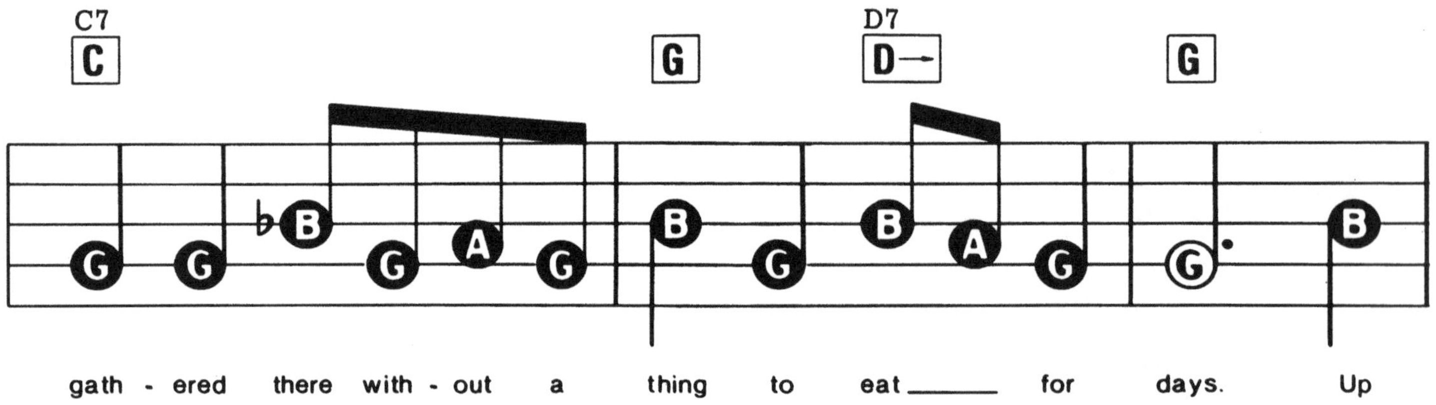

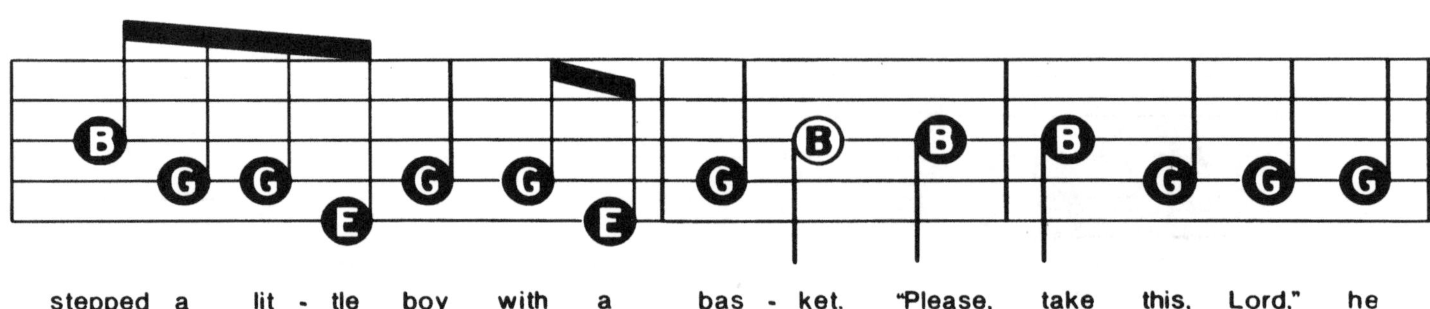

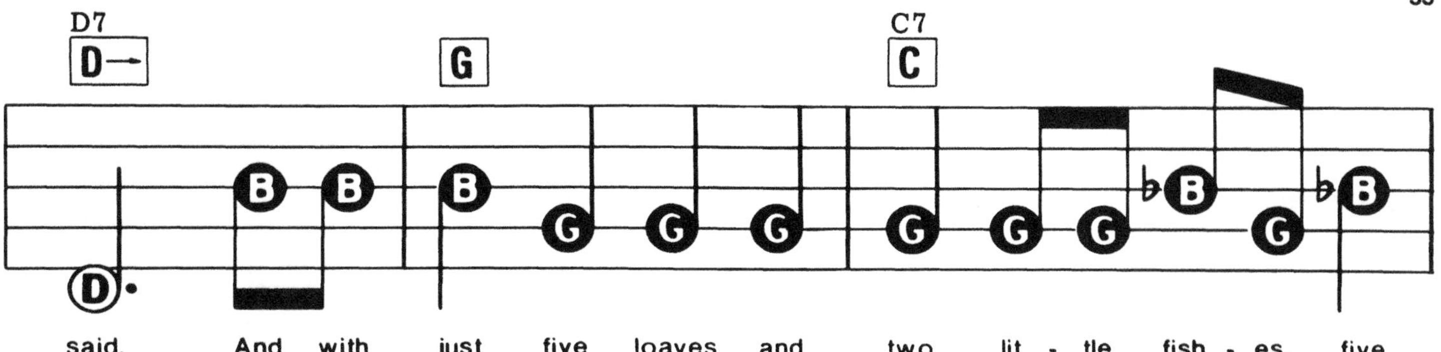

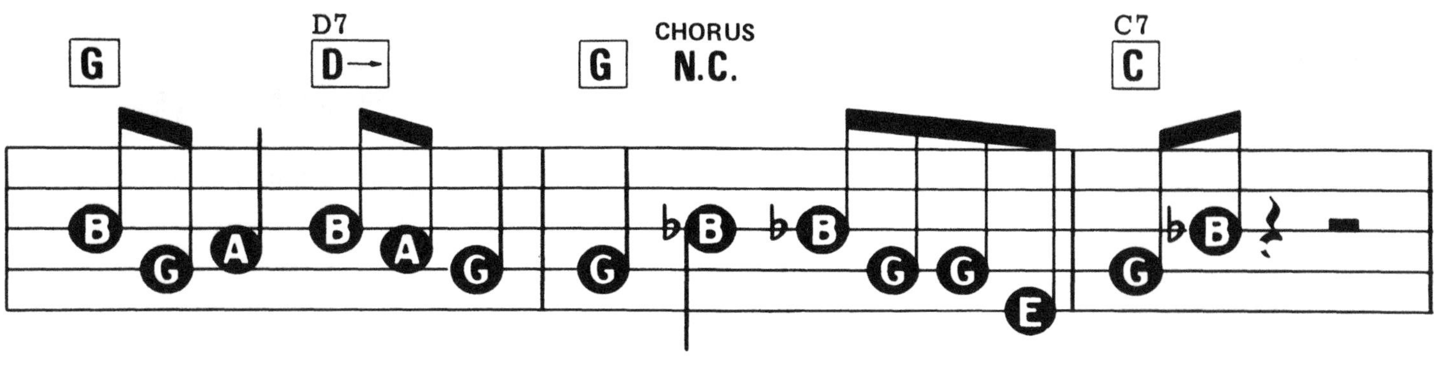

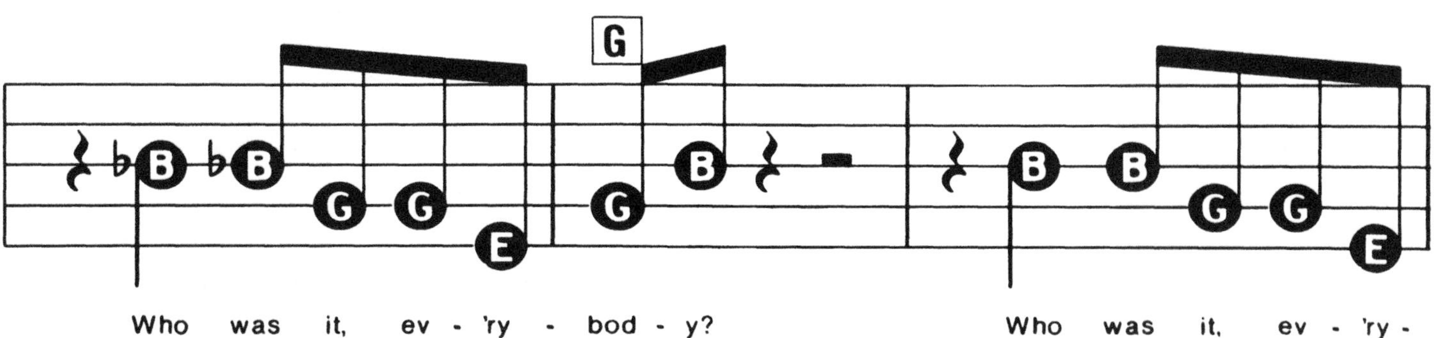

2. Now, pay close attention, little children; it's somebody you ought to know.
   It's all about a Man who walked on earth nearly two thousand years ago.
   Well, He healed the sick and afflicted, and He raised them from the dead.
   Then they nailed Him on an old rugged cross and put thorns on His head.
   CHORUS
3. Well, they took Him down and buried Him, and after the third day,
   When they came to His tomb, well, they knew He was gone for the stone was rolled away.
   "He's not here for He is risen," the angel of the Lord did say.
   And when they saw Him walking with His nail-scarred hands they knew He came back from the dead.
   CHORUS

On The Jericho Road

Registration 7

Words and Music by
Don S. McCrossan

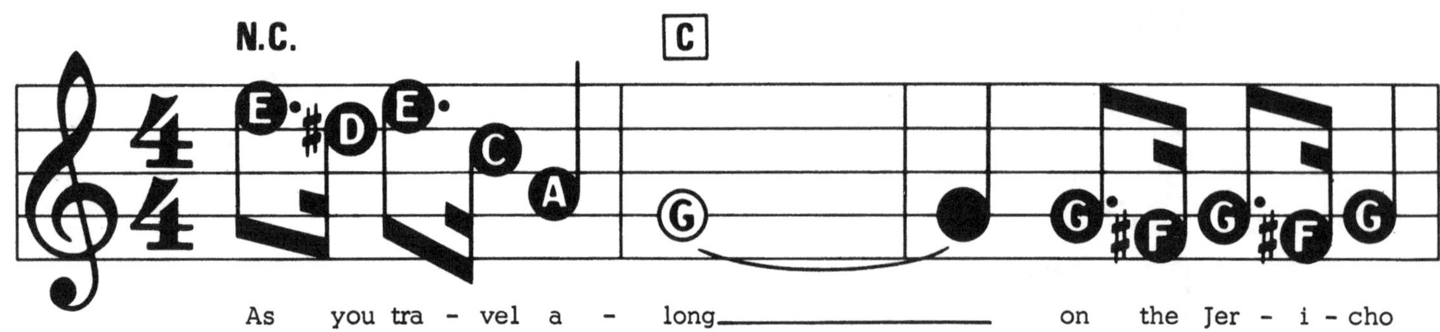

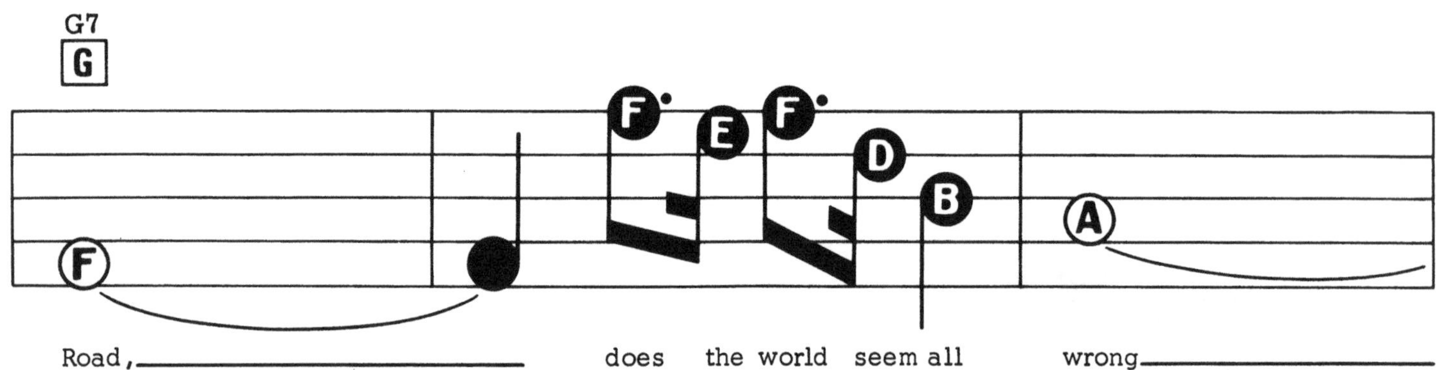

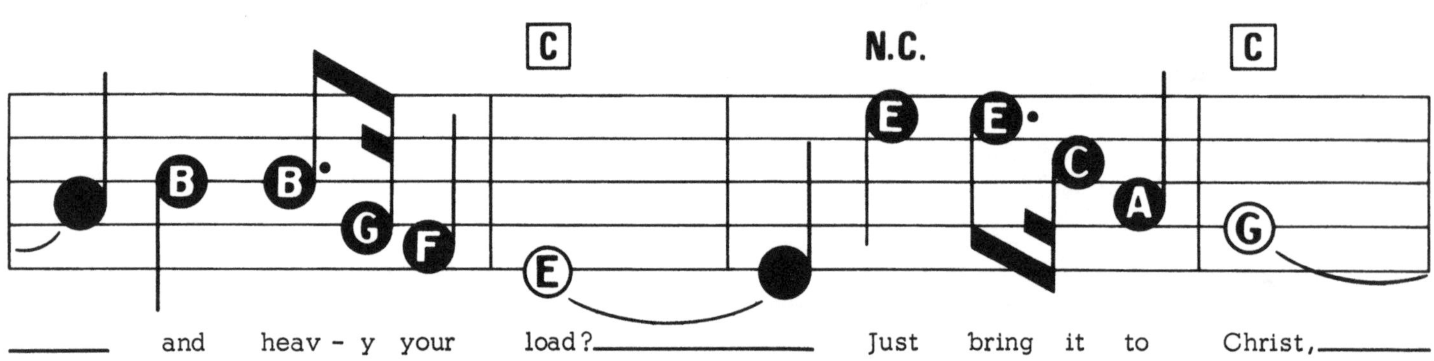

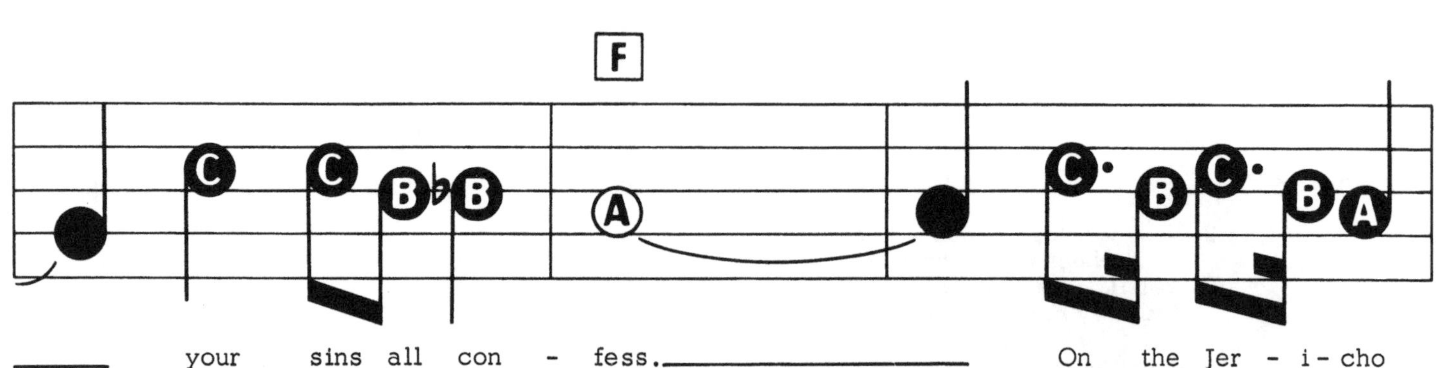

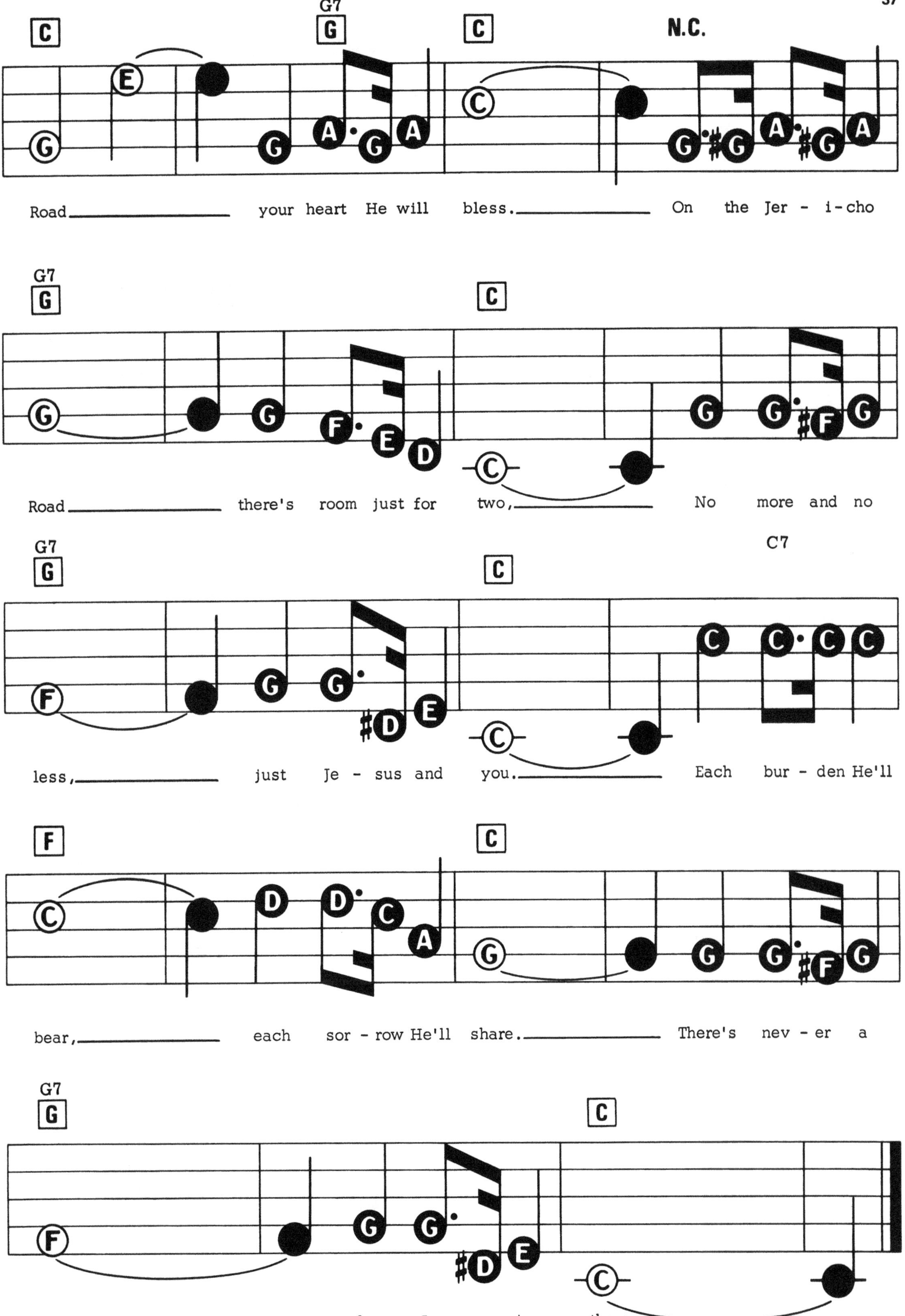
C G7 G C N.C.
Road your heart He will bless. On the Jer - i-cho
G7 G C
Road there's room just for two, No more and no
G7 G C C7
less, just Je - sus and you. Each bur - den He'll
F C
bear, each sor - row He'll share. There's nev - er a
G7 G C
care for Je - sus is there.

How Great Thou Art

Registration 2

By Stuart K. Hine

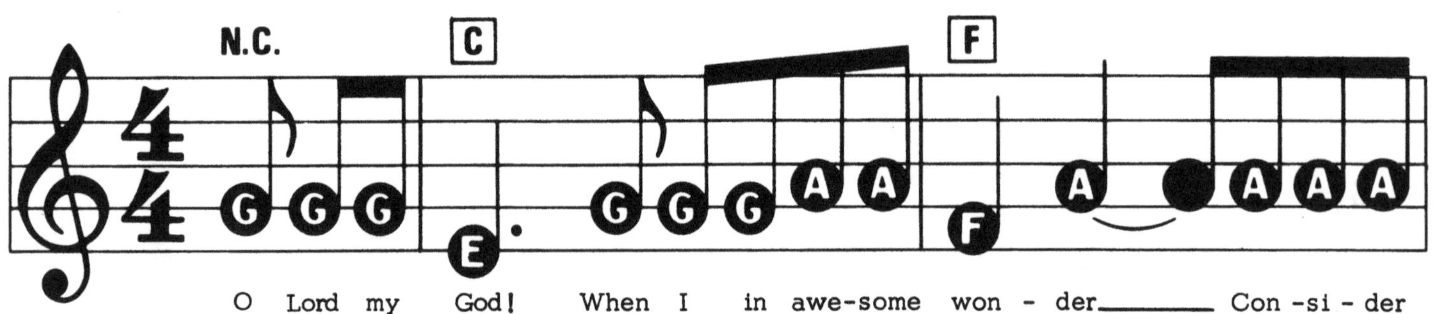

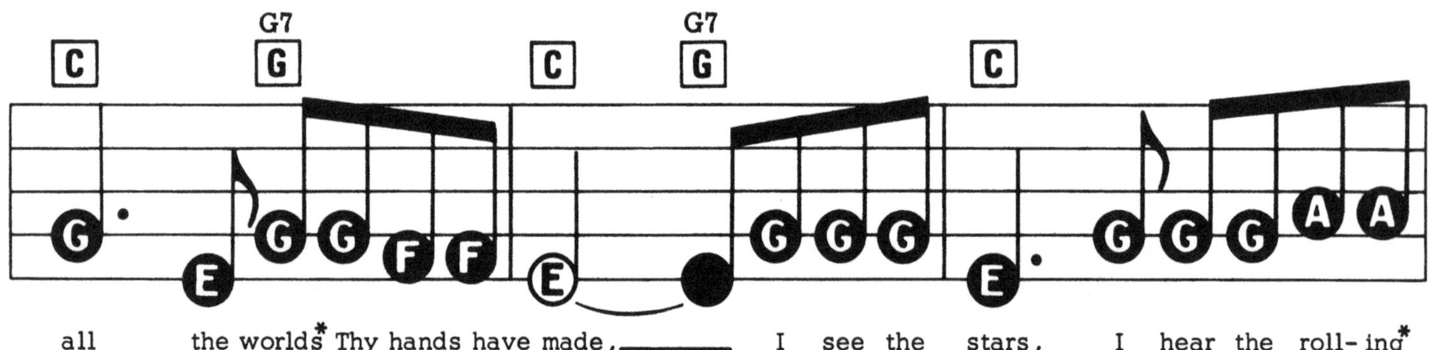

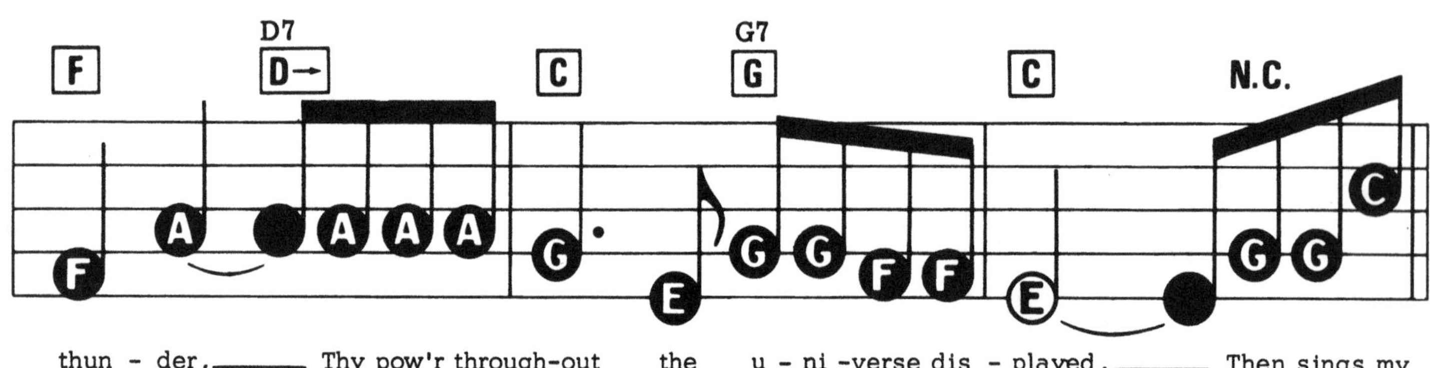

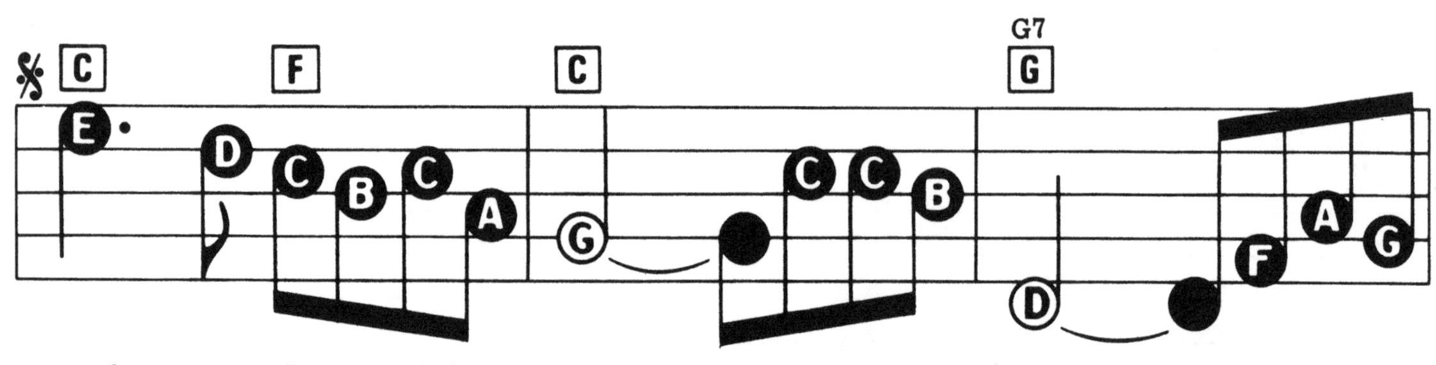

*Author's original words are "works" and "mighty".

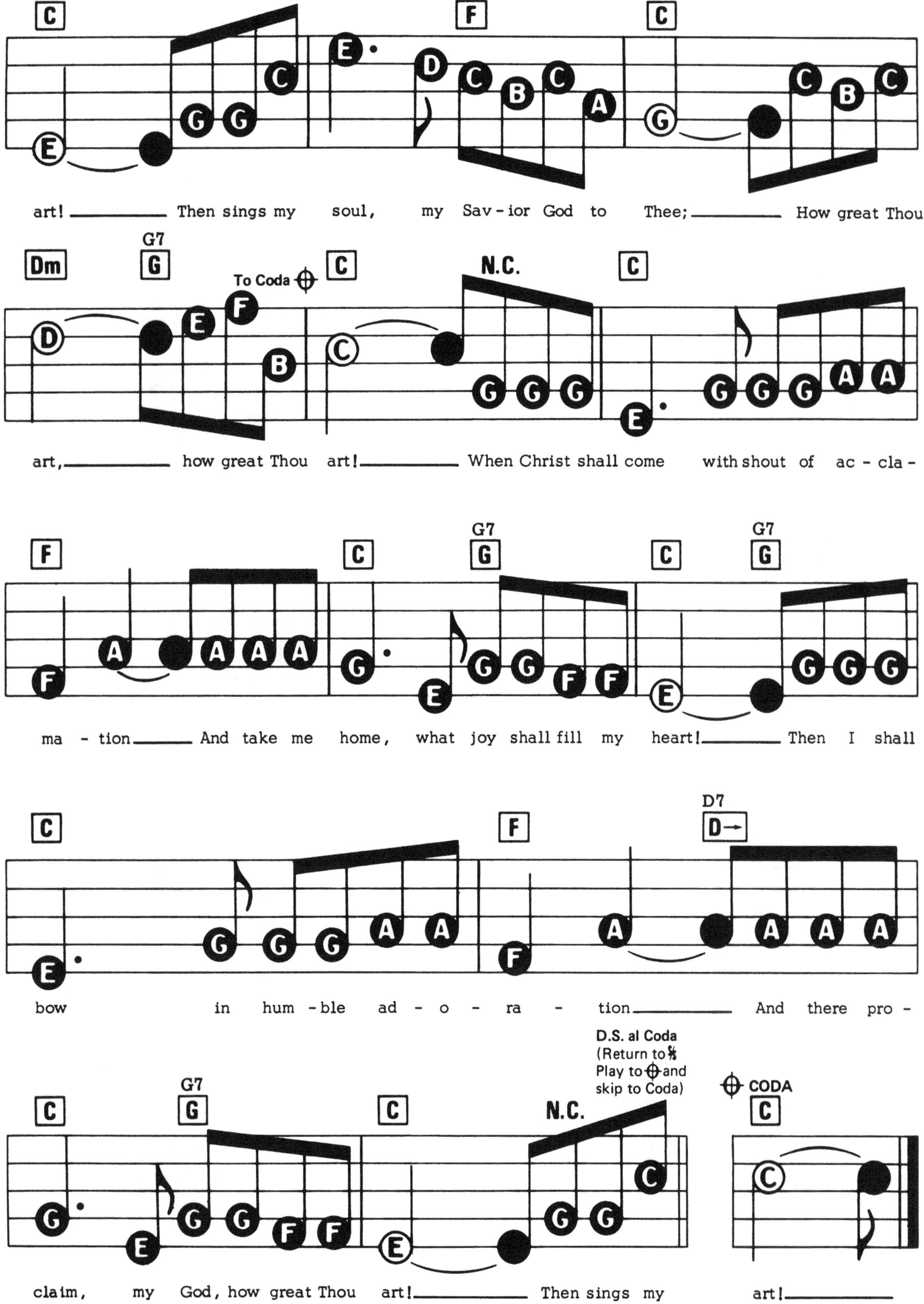
C
F
C
art! Then sings my soul, my Sav - ior God to Thee; How great Thou
Dm
G7
G
To Coda
C
N.C.
C
art, how great Thou art! When Christ shall come with shout of ac - cla -
F
C
G7
G
C
G7
G
ma - tion And take me home, what joy shall fill my heart! Then I shall
C
F
D7
D
bow in hum - ble ad - o - ra - tion And there pro -
C
G7
G
C
N.C.
D.S. al Coda
(Return to
Play to and
skip to Coda)
CODA
C
claim, my God, how great Thou art! Then sings my
art!

Keys To The Kingdom

Registration 3

Words and Music by
Jenny Lou Carson

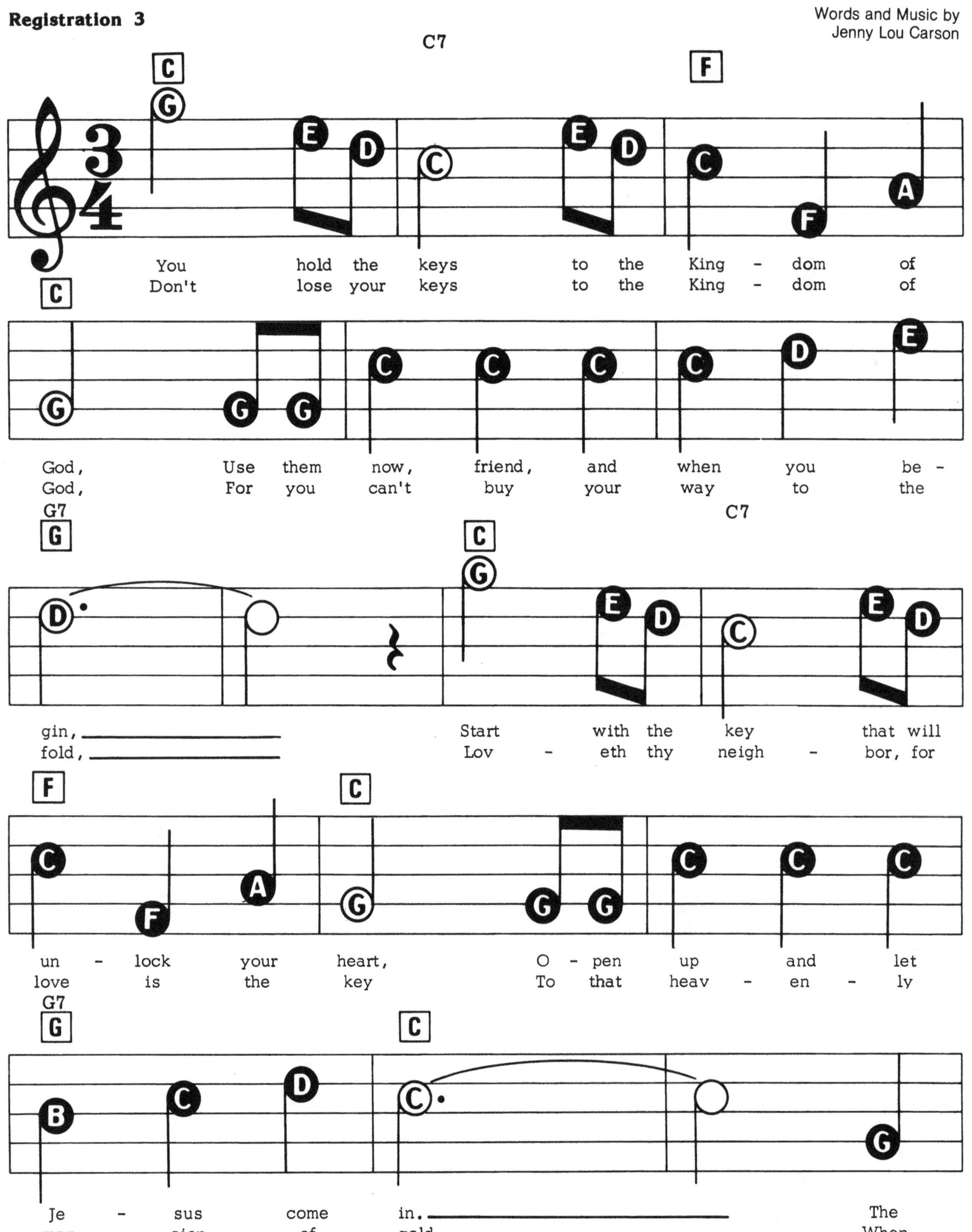

G7
G
C
D D D D C B C E G
mas - ter key's next, my dear neigh - bor, It's
trum - pets ring out in the morn - ing, And
G7
G
C
D D D D C D E
one you should use ev - 'ry day;
you step where an - gels have trod;
C7
F
G E D C E D C F A
Prayer is the key to the great pear - ly
That's the great day you'll be so glad you
C
G7
G
G G G C C C B C D
gates, Yes, you're un - lock - ing them when you
used All the keys to the King - dom of
1
C
G7
G
2
C
C C
pray.
God.

Will The Circle Be Unbroken

Registration 4

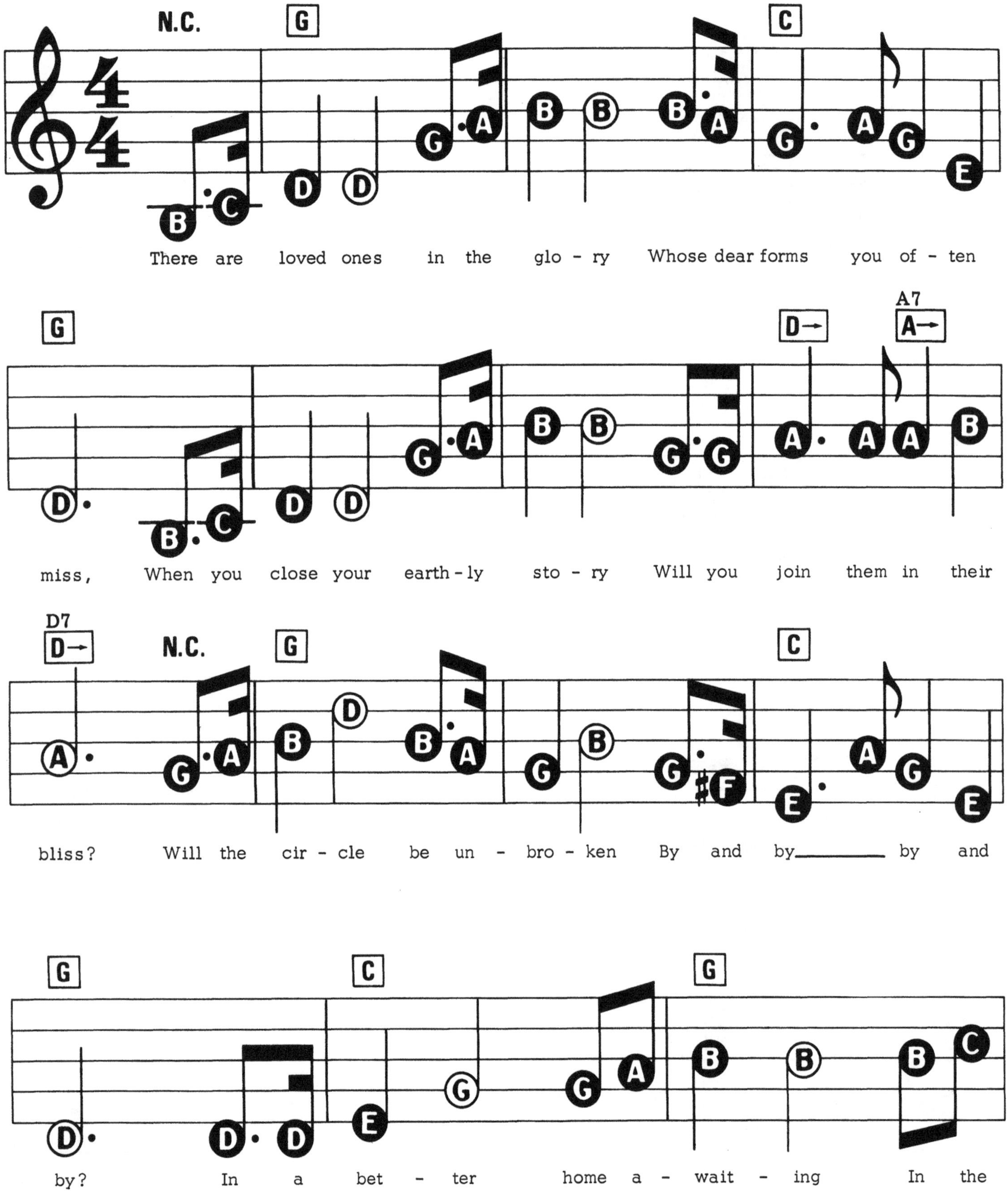

N.C. G C

There are loved ones in the glo - ry Whose dear forms you of - ten

G D→ A7 A→

miss, When you close your earth - ly sto - ry Will you join them in their

D7 D→ N.C. G C

bliss? Will the cir - cle be un - bro - ken By and by ___ by and

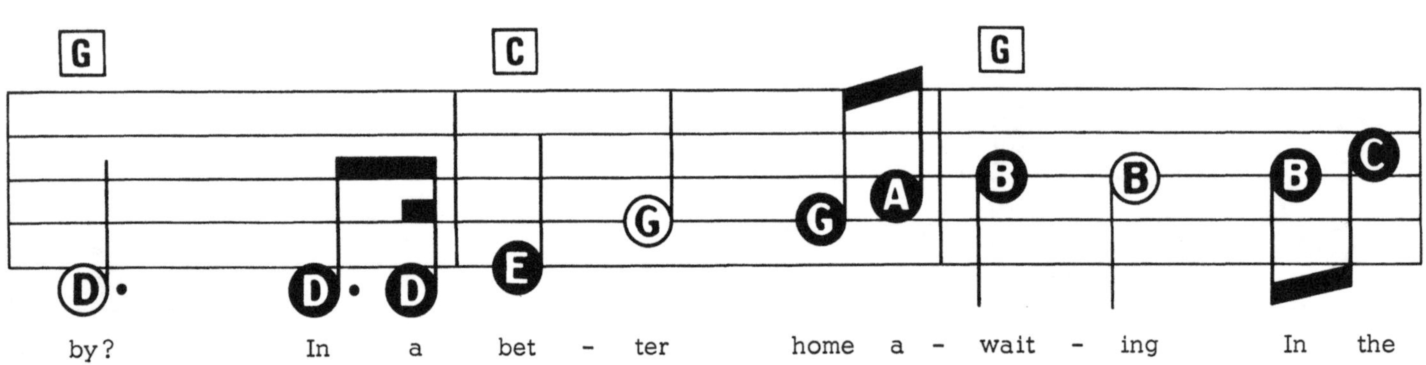

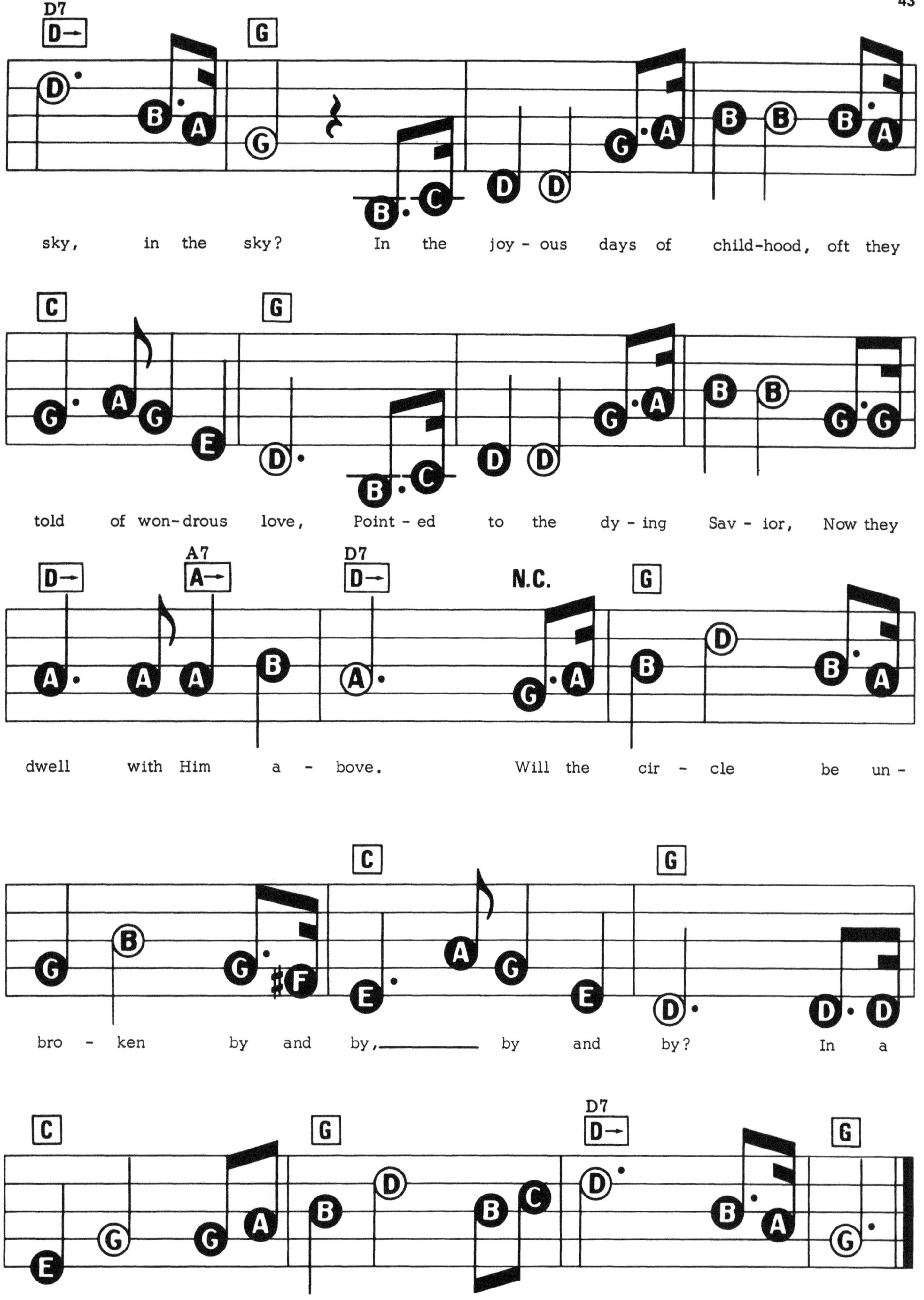
D7 D→ G
sky, in the sky? In the joy - ous days of child-hood, oft they
C G
told of won-drous love, Point - ed to the dy - ing Sav - ior, Now they
D→ A7 A→ D7 D→ N.C. G
dwell with Him a - bove. Will the cir - cle be un -
C G
bro - ken by and by, by and by? In a
C G D7 D→ G
bet - ter home a - wait - ing In the sky, in the sky?

(There'll Be) Peace In The Valley (For Me)

Registration 2

Words and Music by
Thomas A. Dorsey

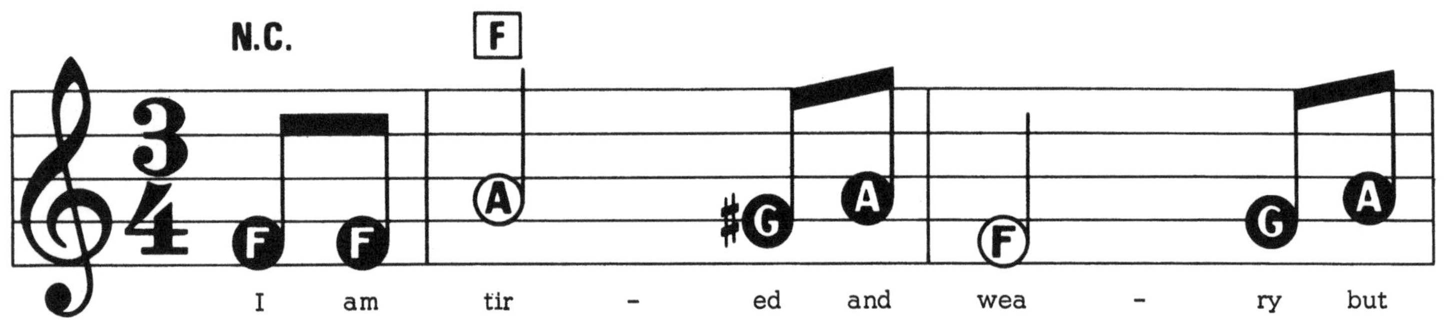

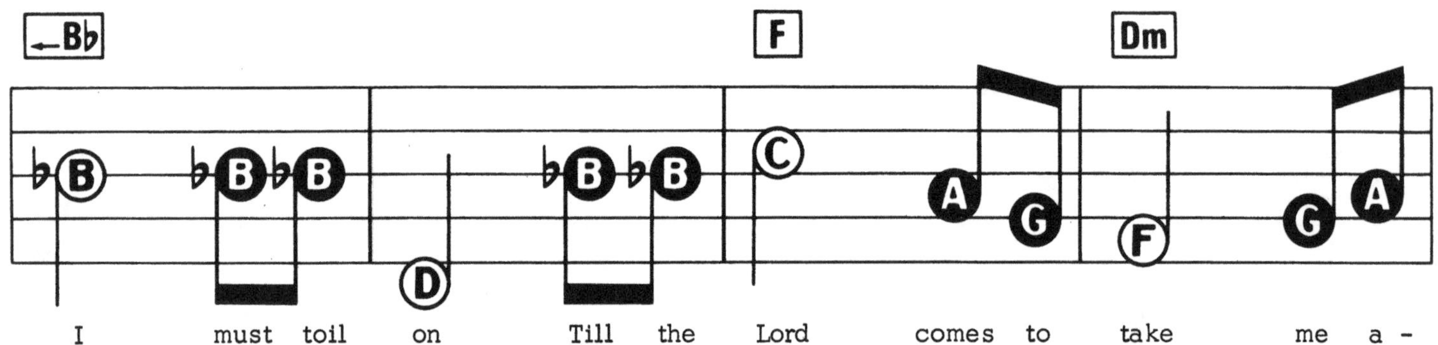

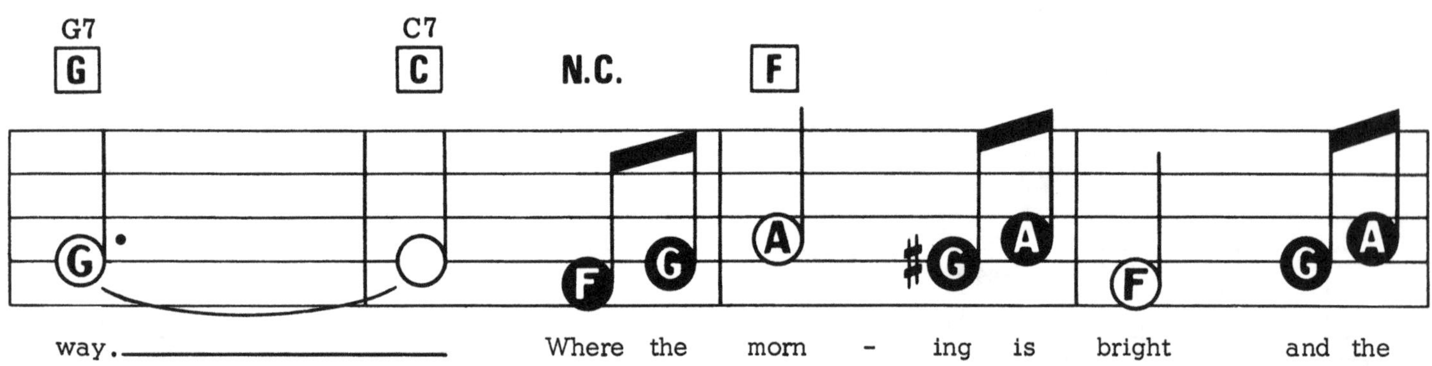

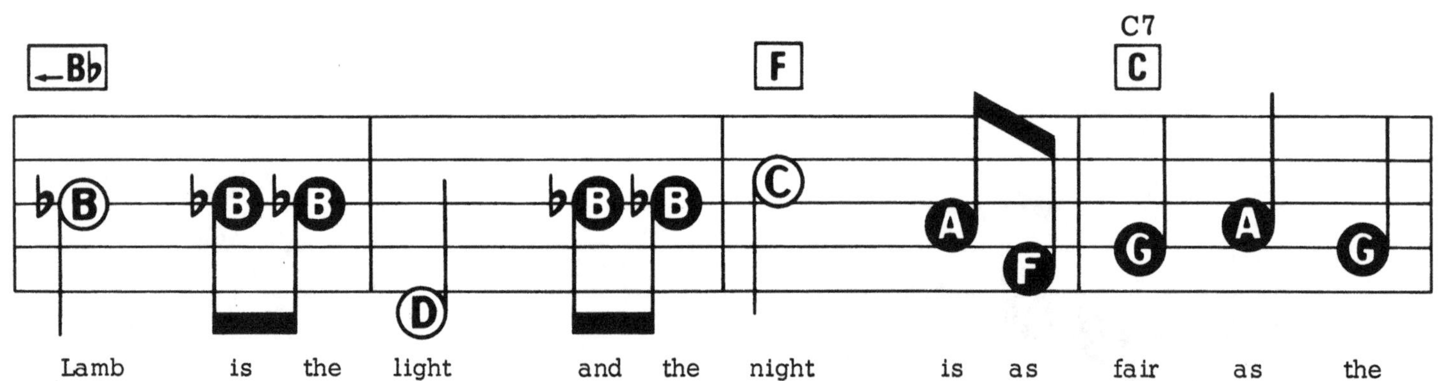

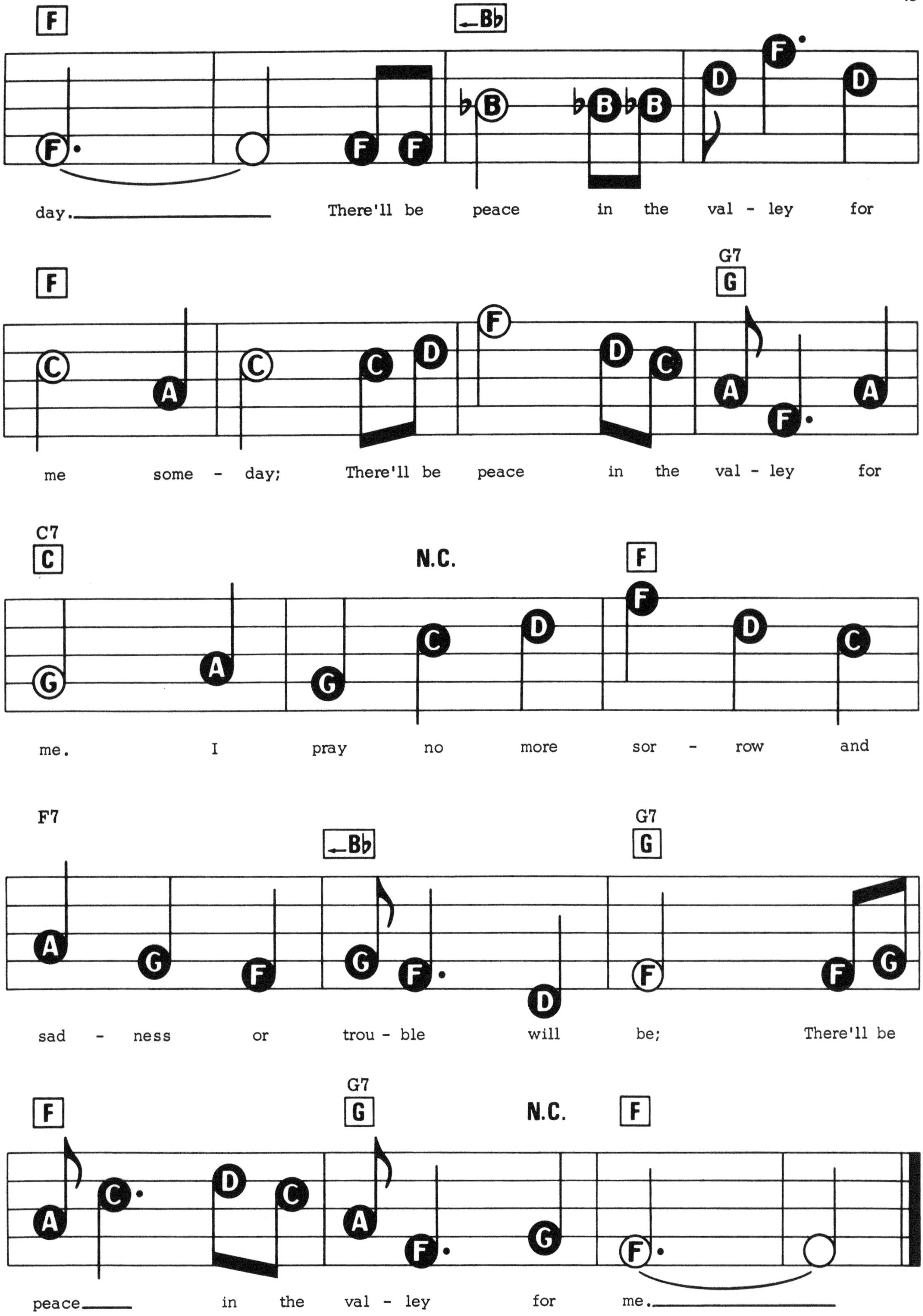

F ←B♭

day.______ There'll be peace in the val - ley for

F G7 G

me some - day; There'll be peace in the val - ley for

C7 C N.C. F

me. I pray no more sor - row and

F7 ←B♭ G7 G

sad - ness or trou - ble will be; There'll be

F G7 G N.C. F

peace___ in the val - ley for me.______

Just A Closer Walk With Thee

Registration 6

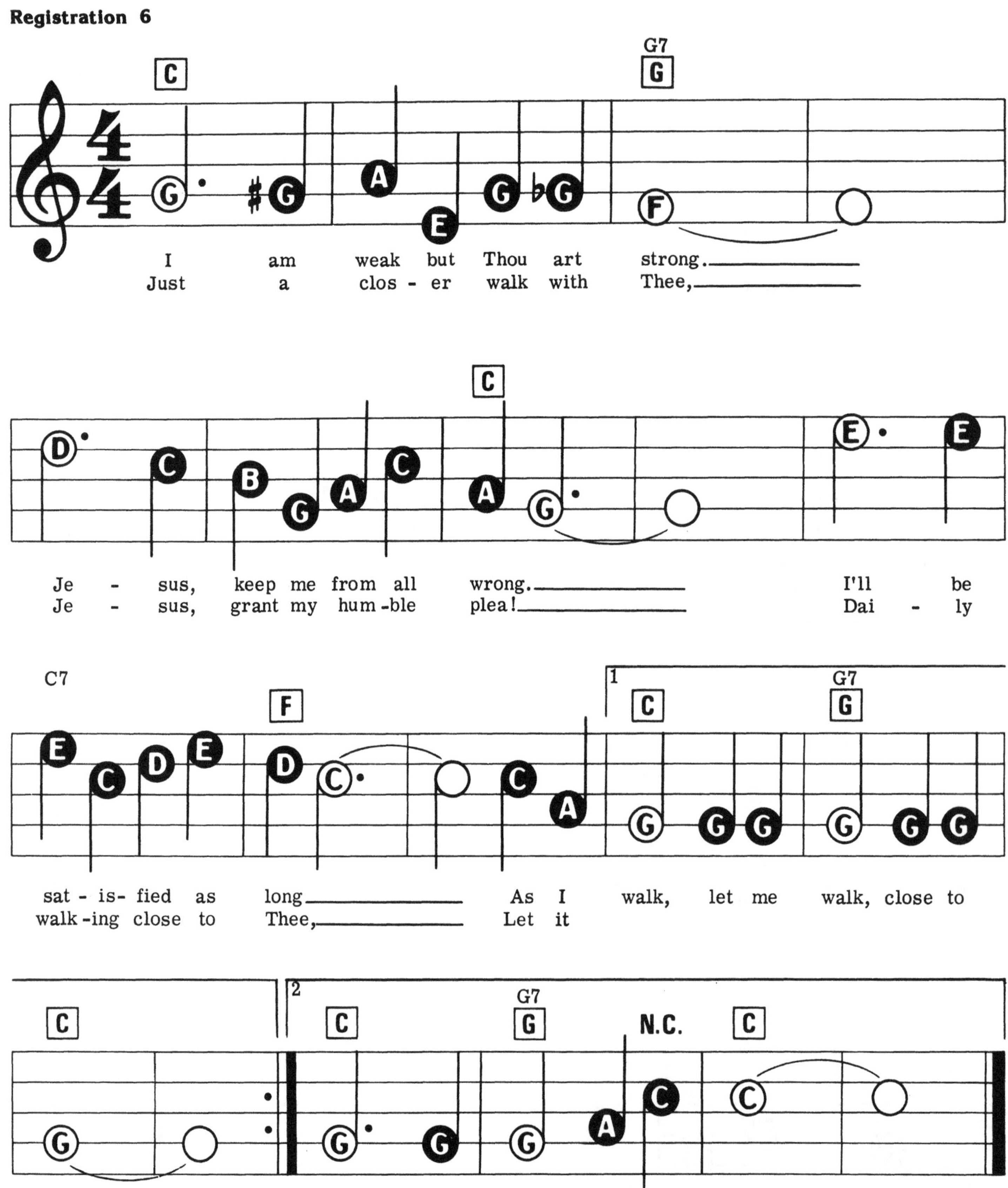

Chord Speller Chart

of Standard Chord Positions

For those who play standard chord positions, all chords used in the E-Z Play TODAY music arrangements are shown here in their most commonly used chord positions. Suggested fingering is also indicated, but feel free to use alternate fingering.

CHORD FAMILY Abbrev.	MAJOR	MINOR (m)	7TH (7)	MINOR 7TH (m7)
C	5 2 1 G-C-E	5 2 1 G-C-Eb	5 3 2 1 G-Bb-C-E	5 3 2 1 G-Bb-C-Eb
Db	5 2 1 Ab-Db-F	5 2 1 Ab-Db-E	5 3 2 1 Ab-B-Db-F	5 3 2 1 Ab-B-Db-E
D	5 3 1 F#-A-D	5 2 1 A-D-F	5 3 2 1 F#-A-C-D	5 3 2 1 A-C-D-F
Eb	5 3 1 G-Bb-Eb	5 3 1 Gb-Bb-Eb	5 3 2 1 G-Bb-Db-Eb	5 3 2 1 Gb-Bb-Db-Eb
E	5 3 1 G#-B-E	5 3 1 G-B-E	5 3 2 1 G#-B-D-E	5 3 2 1 G-B-D-E
F	4 2 1 A-C-F	4 2 1 Ab-C-F	5 3 2 1 A-C-Eb-F	5 3 2 1 Ab-C-Eb-F
F#	4 2 1 F#-A#-C#	4 2 1 F#-A-C#	5 3 2 1 F#-A#-C#-E	5 3 2 1 F#-A-C#-E
G	5 3 1 G-B-D	5 3 1 G-Bb-D	5 3 2 1 G-B-D-F	5 3 2 1 G-Bb-D-F
Ab	4 2 1 Ab-C-Eb	4 2 1 Ab-B-Eb	5 3 2 1 Ab-C-Eb-Gb	5 3 2 1 Ab-B-Eb-Gb
A	4 2 1 A-C#-E	4 2 1 A-C-E	5 4 2 1 G-A-C#-E	5 4 2 1 G-A-C-E
Bb	4 2 1 Bb-D-F	4 2 1 Bb-Db-F	5 4 2 1 Ab-Bb-D-F	5 4 2 1 Ab-Bb-Db-F
B	5 2 1 F#-B-D#	5 2 1 F#-B-D	5 3 2 1 F#-A-B-D#	5 3 2 1 F#-A-B-D

E-Z Play® TODAY Registration Guide For All Organs

On the following chart are 10 numbered registrations for both tonebar (TB) and electronic tab organs. The numbers correspond to the registration numbers on the E-Z Play TODAY songs. Set up as many voices and controls listed for each specific number as you have available on your instrument. For more detailed registrations, ask your dealer for the E-Z Play TODAY Registration Guide for your particular organ model.

REG. NO.		UPPER (SOLO)	LOWER (ACCOMPANIMENT)	PEDAL	GENERALS
1	Tab	Flute 16′, 2′	Diapason 8′ Flute 4′	Flute 16′, 8′	Tremolo/Leslie - Fast
	TB	80 0808 000	(00) 7600 000	46, Sustain	Tremolo/Leslie - Fast (Upper/Lower)
2	Tab	Flute 16′, 8′, 4′, 2′, 1′	Diapason 8′ Flute 8′, 4′	Flute 16′ String 8′	Tremolo/Leslie - Fast
	TB	80 7806 004	(00) 7503 000	46, Sustain	Tremolo/Leslie - Fast (Upper/Lower)
3	Tab	Flute 8′, 4′, 2⅔′, 2′ String 8′, 4′	Diapason 8′ Flute 4′ String 8′	Flute 16′, 8′	Tremolo/Leslie - Fast
	TB	40 4555 554	(00) 7503 333	46, Sustain	Tremolo/Leslie - Fast (Upper/Lower)
4	Tab	Flute 16′, 8′, 4′ Reed 16′, 8′	Flute 8′, (4) Reed 8′	Flute 8′ String 8′	Tremolo/Leslie - Fast
	TB	80 7766 008	(00) 7540 000	54, Sustain	Tremolo/Leslie - Fast (Upper/Lower)
5	Tab	Flute 16′, 4′, 2′ Reed 16′, 8′ String 8′, 4′	Diapason 8′ Reed 8′ String 4′	Flute 16′, 8′ String 8′	Tremolo/Leslie
	TB	40 4555 554 Add all 4′, 2′ voices	(00) 7503 333	57, Sustain	
6	Tab	Flute 16′, 8′, 4′ Diapason 8′ String 8′	Diapason 8′ Flute 8′ String 4′	Diapason 8′ Flute 8′	Tremolo/Leslie - Slow (Chorale)
	TB	45 6777 643	(00) 6604 020	64, Sustain	Tremolo/Leslie - Slow (Chorale)
7	Tab	Flute 16′, 8′, 5⅓′, 2⅔′, 1′	Flute 8′, 4′ Reed 8′	Flute 8′ String 8′	Chorus (optional) Perc Attack
	TB	88 0088 000	(00) 4333 000	45, Sustain	Tremolo/Leslie - Slow (Chorale)
8	Tab	Piano Preset or Flute 8′ or Diapason 8′	Diapason 8′	Flute 8′	
	TB	00 8421 000	(00) 4302 010	43, Sustain	Perc Piano
9	Tab	Clarinet Preset or Flute 8′ Reed 16′, 8′	Flute 8′ Reed 8′	Flute 16′, 8′	Vibrato
	TB	00 8080 840	(00) 5442 000	43, Sustain	Vibrato
10	Tab	String (Violin) Preset or Flute 16′ String 8′, 4′	Flute 8′ Reed 8′	Flute 16′, 8′	Vibrato or Delayed Vibrato
	TB	00 7888 888	(00) 7765 443	57, Sustain	Vibrato or Delayed Vibrato

NOTE: TIBIAS may be used in place of FLUTES.
VIBRATO may be used in place of LESLIE.